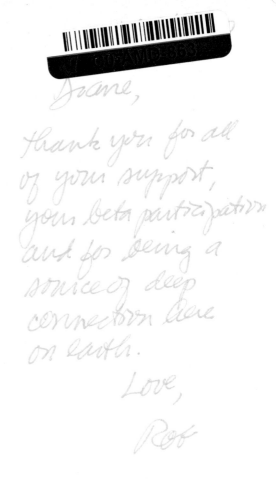

talking with (god)
by Rob H. Geyer

talking with (god)

talking with (god)

OTHER BOOKS BY ROB H. GEYER

Witness of the Heart (1990)

Little Buddha Book Series
Book One   (2017)
Book Two   (2018)
Book Three (2019)

Nine, A Holy Week Story of Love (2019)

talking with (god)

Dedication

In deepest appreciation, I dedicate this book to (god), who I know as Abba (father), Na'a (mother), Yeshiwa (brother) and Lia (sister) and (Love in Action).

I also dedicate this book to my friend, Dan Moore, who believes in me, as I believe in him.

talking with (god)

Appreciation

I want to express my sincere appreciation for the following people who were involved in the creation of this book with me.

Maureen M. Geyer, my wife and best friend, for all of her love, encouragement and support and for her listening to me read this book, giving me space and time to write and for 'making my day' through her praise.

Mary Martinéz, my dear friend, who supplied me with wonderful, thoughtful ideas, served as a sounding board and performed invaluable editing duties, in addition to artwork you will see later in this book.

Cheri Warren, my tech angel and dear friend, who provided all of the keen technical savvy leading to the production for this book. Without her this book would not be in your possession.

Mike (Sketch) Wurman, my trail brother and friend, for the fabulous illustrations on the cover and throughout this book. They are such an important part of what makes this book come alive.

My Beta Test Group, both new and old friends, who provided invaluable assistance to me in the creation of this book. It truly would not be what it is without each and every one of them. They are all *godsends* to me.

Neale Donald Walsch, for his courage to speak his truth and providing the spark for me to do the same.

Dan Baggott, my brother of forty years, whose wisdom and friendship means so much to me and who shared the concept of his "knower" with me.

talking with (god)

Hartwick College, the Religion department there from 1970-1974, especially Dr. Herman Keiter and the Living Learning Center for opening and expanding me and giving me wings to fly.

Bill Stropes, for seeing me for who I was and for being a wonderful boss at the Holiday inn.

Ellie Groel, my friend and my daughter, Jenny's, wonderful college roommate, for her support and for the idea that inspired me to write the poem used on the back cover of this book.

talking with (god)

Preface

I ordinarily don't read the Preface of a book. I'm not sure exactly why. Maybe it's because I want to get started with the main story right away. So, I wondered, is there any point to my writing one? I decided that there was because I have a few things to tell you I think you'll want to know.

I want to establish a relationship with you, the reader. I'm hoping this book comes completely from my heart and that you hear and feel it the same way.

I've been thinking about this book for a quite a while. Part of the reason is that I wasn't sure if anyone would believe me when I told them I've been having intimate two-way conversations with (god) since 1997. That's a very long time. I'm still not completely sure but it's important for me to give you the chance to decide for yourself. If you're reading this, that's a good sign you're open to hearing more.

I put (god) in parentheses because not everyone calls (god) by the same name. There are probably hundreds of names people use when referring to (god) and I wanted to make sure you use the one that feels right to you. So, when you see (god) written in this book, please insert the name that you use.

I also want to mention that I chose to use lower case letters in the title on purpose, hoping that it would encourage you to form a more personal relationship with (god) right from the start. It's more about opening your heart and sharing your life with (god), than it is about abiding by others ideas and concepts that may restrict you. I wanted to ensure the door between you and (god) was as wide open as possible.

I realize this book may not be for everyone, even though I believe it could be. I know every reader can have their own personal, direct, intimate conversations with (god), but I'm pretty sure not everyone wants to. And for some, they may want it, but haven't found a way to believe it is possible, at least not for them. I understand there are lots of reasons people feel this type of conversation is not possible, and that very belief is likely to prevent it from happening.

But for all those who are open to this idea, I want to assure you that it is real. I know this personally because it happens to me every day. The length and depth of our conversations vary, but I know (god) is always present and available to me, just as I know (god) is there for everyone.

Perhaps you need a spark to light you up and get you started. I know I did. I hope this book can be a starting point for you or if you already have a conversational relationship, I hope what you find here helps deepen and strengthen it.

For me, the spark happened one day in 1997 when I found myself in one of my favorite bookstores, circling a display table. A beautiful book cover caught my eye. I picked up the book, glanced through it and set it back down. After wandering around for a while, I ended up back at the same table and was drawn to the same book. I felt a powerful physical attraction, picked up the book once again and knew it was going home with me. That book was Conversations with God: An Uncommon Dialogue by Neale Donald Walsch. As soon as I got to my car I began reading. In it, Neale talks about his personal conversations with God and reveals to the reader the insights he experienced. I was amazed at the depth and breadth of his conversations. I'm indebted to him for his courage, openness and dedication in sharing his experiences with God.

It turned out to be just the catalyst I needed to begin my own journey. I thought to myself, if Neale can have conversations with God, so can I. If he can ask his own questions and receive his own personal answers, so can I.

And so, my own conversations began.

talking with (god)

At the beginning I had many, many questions and more than a few doubts, but some part of me believed it would work, if I gave it some time. I wanted to find answers to some of my most basic questions. I wondered, would (god) really engage with me? From previous experiences, I knew I could talk out loud or say things in my head to (god), but it was another thing altogether to believe I'd receive a direct response from (god).

At times, I wondered if I was worth (god's) time. And, if somehow, I was, would (god) answer all of my questions? I also wondered how long it would take for it to happen.

Beyond these initial questions, I recognized there had been periods in my life when I didn't feel I belonged here on this earth. I'd felt disconnected and uncomfortable in my own skin. Some days when I went for a walk, it even felt as if my feet never touched the ground. So, I wondered, how was it going to be possible for me to connect with (god)? I didn't really know, but I knew I wanted to try.

Perhaps you feel there is some reason that will prevent you from having your own personal conversations with (god). I encourage you to sit back, close your eyes, breathe easily in and out for a few minutes and ask yourself what your heart truly wants. If it is to have a beautiful relationship with (god), you will.

And I am here to help 'nudge' you in that direction, should you want it.

5/21/2020

talking with (god)

Table of Contents

Setting the Stage
(my story)

talking with (god)

It feels important to me to tell you some parts of my story. I'm a North Country boy from the real 'Upstate New York,' having been born in 1952 in Ogdensburg, along the St. Lawrence river, then living in Watertown, on the northeastern edge of Lake Ontario, until I was eight years old. Most people have told me this isn't enough time for a person to live in one area and claim it as their own for life, but I disagree. Maybe that's one thing you should know about me. I tend to stick to my guns.

I had a very happy childhood in Watertown. I lived on a street with lots of friends and had wonderful parents and a close family. I had freedom to roam around my neighborhood and beyond, as long as I was home for dinner. And I took advantage of this to have adventures with my sister or my friends or by myself. I've always been comfortable being by myself and enjoyed hopping on my bike and exploring all of the open spaces around me.

Lots of things were important to my parents and church was one of them. We went to the Presbyterian Church on the main drag in town every Sunday. Thinking about it, all I remember was that the sanctuary was huge, the windows were pretty and I went to Sunday School class. I don't remember one single lesson I learned there. My sister, Alison, the keeper of all of my childhood memories might be able to tell you more. I guess church wasn't that important to me then.

One day, my father came home and told us that we'd be moving very soon to Delmar, New York, a town about 185 miles southeast of us. I didn't like this news. I was happy where I was, thank you very much. I think I got on my bike and rode off. I suppose I came back home after a while, but I'm sure I still wasn't happy. What kid wants to leave all of his friends and have to start all over again?

Well, we did move. And I did start over again in this new place. Fortunately, my bike came with us and I often took off, trying to get lost among these new streets and roads. I never did. I guess

talking with (god)

I have too good an internal navigation system. Funny, but that's applied to many areas of my life. Somehow there's always been some part of me that is connected to something that guides me. I wonder if this applies to everyone, but that we just don't recognize it.

I didn't know it at the time we moved, but this change of location would be an extraordinary event, because I would meet and marry the love of my life, my wife, Maureen. And we would have two wonderful children, Jenny and Tommy. And they would go on to meet their spouses and have their own children. And I wonder, what would have happened if my father had not come home that day and told us we were moving? What a valuable lesson there is in that for me.

But we did move, and as before, we went to church every Sunday. This time, it was the Delmar Reformed Church. Same kind of big sanctuary, same beautiful windows, same Sunday School classes. As I grew older, I ended up staying in the sanctuary longer and was able to hear more of the church service. Our minister, Dr. LeRoy Brandt, had a wonderfully deep resonant voice. He stood on a raised platform, behind an imposing lectern, dressed in a long flowing black robe and spoke in a commanding tone. Whenever he leaned forward to make a strong point, I could feel the fear surround me. He may not have meant for that to happen, but it did. It made me wonder, is this how God felt about me? Was I some sort of threat to God that I needed to be made to fear Him? And it was especially challenging for me when the lessons came from the Old Testament in the Bible, because they seemed absolutely full of fear, anger and vengeance. God was portrayed as justifiably wrathful, because after all, His people had disobeyed Him and therefore would need to be punished. Was it any wonder I was afraid of God? And what would possess me to want to get closer to Him? A better idea seemed to be to stay as far away as possible and see if I could fly under the radar. Of course, I was told that God knew everything, so there was no such thing as

talking with (god)

'flying under the radar' and that I should try to be "good". It's interesting that this belief in the need to be "good" came directly from a teaching of the Reformed Church – that every person is a sinner who needs "salvation". We were taught that salvation, which is the deliverance from sin, cannot be earned, but rather is a wholly unmerited gift from God. And each person's response to this gift should be to do "good works". My intention in sharing this part of my life is not to disparage the Reformed Church or any other church, but to shed some light on how it affected me and the beliefs that I came to adopt (until I didn't).

One day when I was riding my bike through the church parking lot, Dr. Brandt came out of the church's side door. I didn't see him in time to turn and change direction and nearly ran into him. He called out to me, since he knew who I was and I was totally surprised. His voice was warm and friendly and he said, "Hello, traveler, where are you going?" I felt that he liked me. He was smiling and seemed "human". Maybe I wasn't doomed after all. That one exchange altered everything about him for me.

During my Junior and Senior High School days, yes, we had both since there wasn't any such thing as "Middle School", I came to know several other ministers. Each one had their own point of view about church and the focus moved away from the judgmental Old Testament to a more loving New Testament, where Jesus was the central figure. I felt an inexplicable connection to Jesus. He cared about people. He healed them and taught everyone about forgiveness. He sat with "sinners" and spoke to crowds, hungry for his hopeful, loving message. I was taken in by his humanity and his divinity.

I became very active in the church, not because it was expected of me, but because I wanted to be. It fulfilled something in me. More and more, I could see myself someday becoming a minister. And then one day, I approached our current minister and asked what I would have to do to become a minister. He told me that I would have to go before the Consistory, our home

talking with (god)

churches governing body, and I would have to answer their questions and convince them that I was committed to pursuing college and then the Seminary. I would need to explain that I'd received "a call". This is another way of saying that God had spoken to me, to my heart and that He wanted me as his servant. It also meant that God wanted me to become a "minister of the word", and if the Consistory approved me, I would then go to the Classis, the regional governing body of the church and they would repeat the process. If they agreed, I would be considered "pre-ordained" to go to Seminary, once my four-year degree was complete.

I'm sure that I talked with my parents about this, but I honestly can't remember that. I know they were pleased to think that I would follow this path. I probably talked with my friends too, but again, I don't remember that either.

It turns out, I passed and not only would the church support me spiritually, they would support me financially in Seminary. This was a big commitment for them, especially since there were three of us from my church who wanted to purse this course of action.

First, I had to get out of high school and into college. I will share with you that studying, taking tests and playing the role of a student did not interest me in the least. I knew enough to get by and to obtain my high school diploma and that was going to have to be enough for some college, I hoped. As it happens, I visited three colleges and two chose me, neither were my first choice. On one follow up trip to the winning institution, Hartwick College in Oneonta, New York in 1970, I was sitting through an introductory presentation meant to benefit incoming freshmen. We were told that we were the "cream of the crop". That made me wonder, since I had a B minus average at best, what kind of "cream" they were talking about.

talking with (god)

Like probably almost all freshmen, I was pretty unsure about what I'd gotten myself into. I was the last of three roommates to arrive, so I got the top bunk in a room designed for two students. Awesome. I'd enrolled as a Psychology major based on my advisor's advice and signed up for several challenging classes, one of which was a pre-med four credit Anatomy and Physiology course. Who in their right mind would give an unsuspecting college freshman a four-credit pre-med course right out of the gate?

Needless to say, I was not a science major, nor interested in becoming a doctor and received a commensurate D minus, for my troubles, which I have to tell you sends your cumulative average or "cum" into the basement in a hurry. I should point out that during the summer before college, I received my assigned draft number, good for one trip to Vietnam for those with unlucky low numbers or anyone not matriculated into college. My superlative 'D minus', when added to my other classes gave me a 1.90 "cum" and placed me firmly on academic probation. One more semester like that and I would be on a very long plane ride. Unbelievably, this did not sink in and I don't recall being paranoid about it, like I probably should have been.

Here's where my story takes a happy turn. Hartwick offered a one-month class for all students right after the first semester called, "Interdis", short for Interdisciplinary Studies. Of course, we the students, had a different name for it. We called it "Interbliss", because it was a blend of several subjects, none of which were particularly challenging. I signed up for one that sounded like fun, overseen by a Religion professor named Dr. Herman Keiter. I loved this man. He was quirky, intelligent, interested in his students and an easy grader. What's not to like? I got an A, switched majors to Religion and best of all, I dumped my insane Psychology advisor.

Obviously, I took a lot of religion courses and it opened my world. They ranged from classic Christian studies to Buddhism and other world religions and included some unusual courses like Phenomenology, which is difficult to explain, because it is the study of consciousness as experienced from a first-person point of view. I also became involved with yoga. My instructor, Dr. Jordan was very engaging and told us many stories about his life and that of his guru. One story occurred when they were both at an ashram, a monastic community retreat, and Dr. Jordan's guru had locked his room key in his room by mistake. Dr. Jordan said teasingly, "Why don't you just walk through the wall and get it," since this was supposed to be possible for an advanced practitioner of his form of yoga. Dr. Jordan's guru turned to him with a serious face, one he rarely witnessed, and responded, "I gave up that kind of thing because it was too showy and people did not understand it." I believed his story was true and it changed my perception of what was possible.

My inner world, and consequently, my beliefs, were changing rapidly. I felt as if I'd expanded well beyond my Christian upbringing and I started to seriously question whether I could move forward after graduation with my original plan to go to seminary. I believe that after taking two critical thinking classes on the Bible, a decision fully formed inside me. There were far too many inconsistencies for me in what religious traditions proclaimed as the truth and what felt right to me in my heart. The very last thing I wanted to do was to be hypocritical and profess to others something I didn't believe myself. I contacted my church leadership and informed them that I would be terminating my commitment to go to seminary. They were not happy and assigned a minister to my case. He contacted me to investigate the reason for my change of mind and made an attempt to try to convince me that all would be well and that I should continue my studies and keep my decision open. He was appealing to my head, but my decision had already been made with my heart. If you remember the opening paragraph of this section, I think you'll know how I responded. I stuck to my guns.

talking with (god)

Despite a deep interest in my religion courses, I found it almost impossible to force myself to go to my other classes. I preferred to be out in nature exploring the many creeks, the vast trainyards, the Susquehanna river and the surrounding hillsides. Oneonta is situated in a beautiful valley between two parallel ridges that curved in many places. Hartwick College was built on one of these curves and had a spectacular view straight up the valley. From one of my college dorm rooms, I had a view of the opposite hills and often thought of walking over and up to the top of one of them to see what their view was like. One day I decided it was time and set off on my journey. After an hour or two I was part way up a distant hill trying to pick my way to the top. It had clouded over suddenly and turned pretty gray and I stopped to rest in an open meadow for a minute. As I looked up, a hole opened in the clouds and brilliant rays of sun broke through and landed all around me and I heard a voice saying, "my son, in whom I am well pleased". I was awestruck, and felt that I was a part of the light that spread out around me. I can still picture it exactly as it happened. I knew it was God's voice and I knew I was loved beyond anything I'd ever felt before. I hoped one day there would be more to come.

In my senior year I decided to join an experimental program called the Living Learning Center, or LLC, for short. The program took over three floors of one of the older dorms on campus and included freshmen through seniors. We all took common courses, many of which were designed by the core professor group that oversaw the program. There was an enormous amount of freedom and upperclassmen were encouraged to take part in the leadership and teaching of the courses or offer one of their own design that the professors approved. That was a golden opportunity for me. I created a course I called, "Sense Awareness", which focused on the relationship between our senses and our approach to life and facilitated it for two semesters. The group varied from 10-20 fellow students and met each week. It had no professor involvement, other than the reports I turned in to them. I'd never heard of a student being able to teach other students for credit, except in the case of graduate teaching assistants and I was thrilled to be a part of this unique experiment. I had taken a leadership role in our church youth fellowship, but this was many steps ahead of that and gave me real insight about working with people and caring about their "success". I'm still in contact with some of my fellow LLC student friends and share a deep bond with them.

After I graduated, Maureen and I got married and lived in downtown Oneonta, while she finished her senior year at the State University College at Oneonta. I began my working career as a janitor at the Holiday Inn outside of town. I had an early shift and found myself cleaning the public area bathrooms, the bar area, including the disgustingly sticky bar mats and vacuuming the main dining room, among other duties. The best part of the job was, if I got called upon to be the substitute dishwasher - which was pretty often, I could eat some of the food they made in the kitchen. Considering my excessively long hair and goatee, this was 1974 after all, I felt lucky to have the job and worked hard. After a few months, the building maintenance supervisor, Bill Stropes, asked me if I'd like to become a maintenance man and work with him. I was sure it would be nicer than what I was doing and said yes. It was during this time that I became aware of the difference between janitors and maintenance men. Janitors clean things and maintenance men fix things. For me, that was a big difference and I knew I'd like working with Bill. He taught me many things and not just about fixing stuff. One day he told me he wanted me to "walk the grounds", which meant to walk around the whole property and pick up all of the trash laying around. He told me to do a thorough job and sent me on my way with a plastic garbage bag. I thought his request rather odd, because I did this all the time when there wasn't anything else to do, but it was my job, so off I went. When I got to the parking lot at the back of the building, I noticed what appeared to be a crumpled piece of paper jammed into some chicken wire that was meant to catch leaves in the fall. As I got nearer, I could see it was a ten-dollar bill. That was an enormous deal to me. You

talking with (god)

see, at the time, my take home pay was $75 a week. Not much to live on, and this ten-dollar bill would pay for Maureen's and my Saturday night dinner out and a movie and maybe even some popcorn. I knew Bill had stuck it there and wanted me to find it. He knew I wouldn't take the money from him directly, so he found another way. Generosity is one of the things I learned from him.

After a wonderful first year of marriage living in a small apartment on East Street, Maureen graduated and we decide to move back home, where the job market was better. I took two part time jobs, one as Youth Director at First Church in Albany and the other as a part-time teller at the Colonie branch of Albany Savings Bank. It was hard to make ends meet, and I needed to pick one full-time job and see if I could advance. My obvious choice was the bank, so I went full time and within a year was transferred to another branch and promoted to a New Accounts Clerk position. From there I proceeded to learn job after job and was eventually promoted to Branch Manager at our East Greenbush location. For me, customer service and staff development were always the most important things. Establishing relationships with folks who really needed help with their finances and doing it in a friendly way made me feel great. Similarly, taking an interest in my coworkers, and wanting them to succeed, became a lifelong focus for me. It took some time, but most of my staff finally came to believe me when I said that I was more interested in their personal development and future life than in their future at the bank.

During my years with the bank, Maureen and I started our family, which accounts for two of my all-time favorite days, the births of our children. Being a husband and father is an incredibly rewarding experience. Caring for and helping raise our daughter and son was wonderful and challenging, and I am so glad to be a part of their lives. Patching up skinned knees, playing on the floor together, going on vacations, assisting with homework, standing near enough to help when relationships with their friends went sideways -- but not so close that they felt smothered, and all of the other things that happen in family life gave me a sense of connection and purpose. And a great deal of problem-solving practice.

Adding in all of the other challenges and events in life, I found myself in the midst of an enormous juggling act. I found it difficult to balance the responsibilities of being a husband, father, son, brother, friend, boss, employee and so many other relationships and it sometimes became overwhelming. And things would pile up, if I let them. I wondered to myself, how are Maureen and I going to pay for our house, work around both of our jobs, manage our finances, pay for college and a wedding and hopefully have something left over for our retirement? I know I am not alone in these thoughts and that everyone faces things like this or something just as challenging, perhaps even more challenging, like a significant health crisis. From my conversations with others, it's readily apparent to me that life offers unlimited opportunities for each of us and that, at times, we all need help. And the challenges aren't restricted to intellectual ones that you can hopefully solve with your mind. There are physical, emotional and spiritual challenges as well. I often wondered, where exactly is all of the help I need going to come from?

Many people find the help they need from religion and a church life. When we moved back to Delmar, Maureen and I returned to Delmar Reformed Church. We were both actively involved and went every Sunday, bringing our children with us. It was a wonderful church and I felt connected to the people there, many of whom I'd grown up with. But, as far as it speaking to my heart, it didn't. For me, there was an emptiness underneath the surface of what was being taught. I couldn't feel (god's) presence. I tried over and over to get something out of the Sunday services, but it was the same every week and I didn't experience any relief or inspiration. I know our church was a wonderful experience for others and I respected and appreciated that, but for me all I felt

talking with (god)

like was a good soldier, marching in and out of the front doors, but never being filled with any real hope or spiritual connection. Despite this, I was very active in the leadership of the church and thought that perhaps this would make up for the lack of spiritual connection and that I could find value and worth in being a part of the church in this way. It did provide connection to people, but not to (god), at least not for me. Perhaps, I'd find what I was looking for in my work.

After many years as a branch manager in several locations, I was promoted to a Regional Branch Coordinator position and oversaw all phases of branch operations for twenty branches and 250 employees. As you can imagine that was challenging and required a steep learning curve on my part. Much of my job centered around problem resolution, whether it was for our customers, our staff or management. I was good at it. However, at times, I wondered, what about me? Was I good at solving all of my own problems? The answer was, yes, most of the time, but not always. There were many times I could have used more clarity and wisdom. But where was this going to come from? And, how was I supposed to find it on my own? I'd come to learn not all problems are the same. Some required the mind, while others required the heart. Was I good at both kinds? No, not always.

And then one day, I found myself in one of my favorite bookstores, circling a display table and a beautiful book cover caught my eye. Yes, this is when I found Neale's book, Conversations with God: An Uncommon Dialogue. Right in the middle of my complicated, normal life.

You may be wondering, what has all of this personal history got to do with this book I've written titled, *talking with (god)*? I would have to say, it has everything to do with it. There isn't one part of my life that hasn't been immeasurably changed by my personal conversational relationship with (god). Part of me wishes that I had always had this, even as a child or perhaps, especially as a

talking with (god)

child. I imagine how different my life might have been if I was able to have my own conversational relationship with (god) and ask all of my own questions and receive all of my own answers.

Through my conversations with (god), that's what I've found and that's what I'd like to share with you now. I'd like to tell you about how my relationship with (god) evolved, because I believe there is wisdom here that will mean something to you. And later, in the section titled, Opening the Door (our story), I'll share a process you can use, to begin or enhance your own personal, direct, intimate conversational relationship with (god).

After reading Neale's book I was convinced that *he* was having a deep and personal conversation with (god), and that it was up to me to decide what *I* wanted. If I truly wanted this same relationship, what would I need to do? For him, it seemed to be, being honest and saying what was really going on in his life. I could do that, couldn't I? Part of me wondered, would (god) talk back to me? Of course, I could tell (god) whatever I wanted, but that didn't mean (god) would respond. In the end, there was only one way to know for sure, I had to start talking.

I began with easy questions. Unfortunately, somehow, I don't have my journals from anything prior to 2011, so I can't tell you what my first set of questions were. That probably doesn't matter anyway. I do remember they were "meatballs" lobbed over the plate, which for those of you who didn't play baseball or softball, means they were the easiest pitches to hit, at least that's what my friends and I called them. They came in slow and went out fast with the crack of the bat. Something like, "(god), if I ask you a question, will you give me an answer?"

I remember that I was quite formal in my approach. Foolishly, I labeled my part with an (R) for Rob and (god's) responses with a big (G), as if I couldn't tell the difference. I think that was funny, even to me at the time, but it's what I decided. Maybe I felt it was respectful and I wasn't going to take any chances in (god) feeling

13

talking with (god)

"dissed" (disrespected) by me. Perhaps, it was just a part of my cultural training and good clear journaling.

For every question I asked, there was almost always an answer. It was as if I knew what to write and I only had to let the pen go. As I thought about it though, a different question formed in my head, was I really talking with (god) or my own imagination? How could I know for sure? That question would not be answered convincingly until later in the relationship. But, the nature of the answers was often beyond my thinking mind's ability to provide, so I figured, what difference does it make, if I feel better because of the conversation? So, I kept going.

The vast majority of my conversations were based on some need I had for greater insight and they remained formal in nature, which I think limited the depth of the responses. At one point, my concern -- really my desperation for an answer, pushed me to open up and speak more truthfully. I was completely honest and expressed how I really felt. It was hard being this vulnerable, but I discovered that honesty is the key for a 'real' conversation.

Sometimes I asked for something specific and received what I'd requested. Sometimes I wouldn't get anything, other than a sense that (god) was listening. Wouldn't mathematical probability suggest this would be true, where no matter how many questions you asked, some would seem to be answered. Sort of like the expression, "even a broken clock is right twice a day."

But there were enough deep conversations, where I experienced peace, calmness and clarity, that I wanted to continue. So, I kept taking baby steps and gained comfort in speaking what was true for me, what was really in my heart. That's when (god's) answers began to blow me away. Not every time, but often enough that I wanted to spend a lot of time in (god's) presence. And the answer to my original question of whether I was truly speaking with (god) or summoning answers from my imagination became

talking with (god)

quite clear, because many of the issues I discussed with (god) were particularly problematic for me and I had not been able to resolve them on my own, no matter how hard I had tried. Everything I tried failed, sometimes miserably, but the answers I began receiving from (god) were clear, practical, understandable and proved amazingly useful. They were far beyond what even my imagination was capable of. Sometimes, the answer itself was proof enough, because it dove deep below my surface and explained *why* I was feeling the way I was and addressed the *root cause* of my dilemma, which gave me the ability to change my perceptions and see things differently. What a fantastic relief.

I did find that it was necessary for me to quiet my mind and my body in order to hear (god's) voice. I struggled a lot with this. When your life focus has been using your mind, it's pretty hard to shut it down, no matter what the motivation is. I'd been taught that the intellect was my primary tool to navigate this world. I think that was a large contributor to the difficulty I had in slowing down and trusting some other source for my answers. I found that it was necessary for me to suspend my mind and move into my heart to hear (god's) voice clearly. Afterward, I could filter what I received through my mind if I wanted a more intellectual version of the truth.

There were numerous times when I received an answer and felt I needed to test it to see what would happen. The answer alone was not self-evident and at times I had to see for myself how things would work out if I ran with what I'd received. Part of me still wanted practical solutions and proof. I bet you can guess which part of me this was. Later, this whole issue of proof would provide one of the most satisfying conversations in my relationship with (god), because it represented a turning point for me. More on this at the end of this chapter.

Another way I came to believe fully in the truth of my conversational partner being (god) was a "knowingness" I felt. A dear friend of mine had often said to me that his proof about his

talking with (god)

conversations with (god) being real was that "he knew it in his knower", which was that part of him that understands and accepts, that *feels* the truth, without needing or wanting any logical or explainable confirmation. He just *knew it*. It took me awhile, but I've come to understand and agree completely with his statement.

At the beginning, the (G) for (god) was a masculine voice and it felt like a father's voice, not my human father and certainly not the "Father" from my religious upbringing. The voice was calming, patient, loving, ready to listen at any time and would always wait to respond until I was done talking (writing). The more this voice spoke, the more obvious it became to me that it was the voice of 'Abba', a heavenly father who cared about me and wanted all good things for me. Abba's love showed through every word and feeling, and I began to trust more and open up. Our relationship shifted from one of formality, to one of intimacy. I could say anything I needed to and I would be accepted. I'm pretty sure I still watched what I said and how I said it, but I believe Abba would have allowed me the freedom of full expression.

This relationship went on for years until one day I sensed a change in (god)'s presence and responses to my questions and statements. It was subtle at first, taking quite a while to become pronounced. I felt a strong feeling of feminine energy within the voice, which surprised me. I wondered about this. My cultural training had not prepared me for sensing the feminine side of (god), so it took me some time to understand (with my mind) and then to embrace (with my heart) this beautiful divine energy. I knew it was "mother" -- again, not my human mother, nor any biblical mother energy, but a wholly, purely divine, spiritual mother. As we began conversing, it became apparent to me that I needed a name which felt right to me. I have always felt a very strong affinity for Native American culture and traditions. As a child growing up in the 1950's, my sister and I watched a ton of Westerns (movies and TV shows) and she and I would root for the Indians to win, which was not a popular decision at the time. They never did of course. I knew, deep in my heart and in my blood (later discovering there is some Native American heritage in me) that the feminine energy had this quality, so I searched for her name, believing I would know it when I found it. After doing some research I came across the name Na'a, which is the Blackfoot tribes' word for "mother" and that felt absolutely right to me.

My conversations were now exclusively with Na'a, which while different, had the same sense of intimacy and the same loving, caring, connective feeling. I think Na'a opened a new part of me and I began to speak more freely about my feelings and it became easier for me to share my deepest concerns with her. One other change that happened was that Na'a asked me questions. I wasn't used to this, because this was rare for Abba. So, I wondered, why the change? What I found was that I experienced far more depth to the conversation when I spent time answering her questions. It made me move beyond my normal thinking mind and into the heart of my feelings. I wasn't used to this and nothing in my life had prepared me for it. As I mentioned, I was trained, meaning that I'd been conditioned to value my intellectual abilities, and to essentially ignore my feelings -- or at least to subjugate them. And along came Na'a to burst that bubble and show me a completely different version of the truth.

There was one great similarity that Abba and Na'a shared in their conversational style and content. Neither of them ever *told* me what to do. They practiced the art of deeply listening to me. Abba often rephrased my thoughts and words reflecting them back to me so I could see them more clearly, while Na'a asked probing questions, giving me the opportunity to recognize the truth for myself. One of my lifelong consistent and fundamental traits is the absolute dislike for anyone telling me what to do. I feel like I was born with this. Nothing gets to me faster than when I'm faced with this issue. I find it fascinating, revealing and so

talking with (god)

rewarding that (god), in whatever form (god) appears, knows this about me and chooses a wise path into my being, never creating a conflict by going against my grain. That, to me, is a very loving gesture.

Another similarity that Abba and Na'a have in common is that our conversations provide me with the opportunity to say anything I am feeling or thinking, all within the safety of a loving relationship. I can allow myself to be open, so that I hear and receive the wisdom they share with me, always knowing I can make all of my own decisions. They are both always open, encouraging and loving and are never judgmental and never say anything unkind to me. In fact, in all of the years we've been speaking, (god) has never uttered one harsh word to me. Firm at times, yes, because I needed that in order to move forward in my life, but never harsh or critical. This is one further way I can tell that I am speaking with (god), rather than any part of *me*. I have plenty of experience recognizing my inner ego voice, which seems to take unnecessary pleasure in making me feel judged, unworthy and insignificant. (Maybe you've heard this same voice inside your head a time or two.) For me, it's become pretty easy to tell the two voices apart.

Over the course of time my conversations would alternate between Na'a and Abba and this felt natural to me. I don't ever remember feeling disappointed with who chose to speak to me. It always felt right. I also found it didn't matter what mood I showed up with, I always felt cared for. Sometimes I was angry, sad, worried, afraid and sometimes I expressed my disappointment in (god). Occasionally, my words were unkind and I ranted for a while telling (god) in no uncertain terms what I thought of (god) and this world. It never mattered to (god). (God) knows I am human. My behavior neither surprises nor upsets (god). These are human feelings. I often supposed that (god) felt and reacted to life the same ways I do. But my conversations have allowed me to "know" that this is clearly not the case and I am extremely grateful for this. Imagine if (god) were to hold some impossibly

18

high standard that no human could meet? What would our lives be like then? Actually, this is what many traditional religious groups believe, but it is not what I've ever experienced in my relationship with (god). This is one of the great truths I've discovered, that how we see life and what we believe is entirely up to each one of us to decide. I consider this an enormous blessing.

One day, when I began a new conversation, there was a new voice in return. It was masculine, soft and yet powerful and comforting. I recognized it immediately as belonging to "Yeshiwa", which is the Aramaic name for Jesus, from the language he spoke. I remember that ever since I was a child, I've always felt a kinship with Yeshiwa. I saw him as the loving presence of (god), who came to earth to spend time sharing a message of love with everyone. My conversations with Yeshiwa were different and somehow allowed me to talk even more freely, especially about personal issues and concerns. I felt Yeshiwa understood my humanness and could respond from a place of unique connection, because of the time he'd spent living here on earth. His voice encouraged me to say whatever was important to me and ask any and all of my questions. Speaking with Yeshiwa was like talking with a brother. I don't have any genetic brothers, but I do have and have had many "brothers" in my life.

I looked forward to my conversations with Yeshiwa, to feeling his warmth, love and support. And as with Abba and Na'a, there continued to be no judgment, no commands to obey, no expectations to fulfill. I have to admit, I am the one with all of the judgments and expectations. I am the one who sometimes speaks harsh words, is impatient and is occasionally angry. But then again, I am the one who lives in this world and who has grown up in this culture and who has adjusted to many of its ways and I can't help but bring all of this with me to every conversation, whether I mean to or not. It is I who want things to be a certain way and become upset when it isn't how I want it to

talking with (god)

be. *I am human*. Yeshiwa knows this and understands this. I believe that he spent real time here, living among people, walking, talking, eating and feeling what it feels like to be human. In a way, who could possibly understand me better?

Yeshiwa was always there for me, and it felt that he just wanted to spend time with me. No agenda, hidden or otherwise. He did not need anything from me. He treated me with kindness and care and deeply listened to me. I felt a profound, often overwhelming sense of love, which changed me as a person in so many ways. Being with him felt precious and wonderful. It still does.

Abba, Na'a and Yeshiwa each have their own voice and their own ways of offering me their insight, but it is always up to me to choose my own path. I never feel they are upset with me for the choices I make, even the ones which contradict their wisdom. I am honored and valued and my path is always respected.

What I've found to be true is that I am sometimes the one who is stubborn, impatient and difficult, so I am the one who is making my life harder than it needs to be. I've come to realize that there is an easy way and a hard way to go through life and I'm far less tempted to choose the hard way now that (god) helps guide me and offers wisdom and powerful insights, making it possible for me to choose more wisely.

After many years of conversing with Yeshiwa, I noticed a shift and a new voice emerged. It was not one I recognized or expected. There was an ethereal quality to it and a feeling of feminine energy, soft, soothing and loving in a new way. I had a sense of something, but couldn't identify it and it remained just beyond my awareness. It felt very mysterious. It was like trying to see the wind. I couldn't see it, but I could definitely feel it and then I knew the voice and a name came to me. Her name was "Lia", which stands for "love in action". Hers is the voice that comes most often now and she is the one who graces me with

talking with (god)

constant love. She is my "sister" spirit, making my divine relationships complete with father, mother, brother and now, sister. And I could see that the progression of the faces and voices of (god) meant something.

Father/Abba arrived so that I could build on a familiar concept and then over time shifted to a new truth, helping me evolve.

Mother/Na'a arrived in my heart, opening me, adding beautiful depth and creating trust and hope.

Brother/Yeshiwa connected with me on a very personal human level, offering practical wisdom, guidance and insight, helping me navigate this magnificent earth life.

Sister/Lia lives fully inside, carrying me, speaking always to my heart, offering me strength and covering me with love.

I can speak with whichever voice feels most right to me at the time. No matter whose voice I hear, I feel loved, even when things are not, in my opinion, going the way I'd like them to. And if I become quiet and listen, Mother/ Father/ Sister/ Brother always comes and talks with me and I know that I am loved.

At some point during my conversations an interesting twist occurred. Not only did I experience different voices from (god), but I noticed different voices from within myself. It's hard to explain exactly. At first it seemed there was only *Me,* which felt mostly "spiritual", but I recognized there were other dimensions to *Me.* It became apparent that there were several strong voices that wanted to be heard. There were voices that spoke from my physical, emotional, mental, spiritual and ego selves. On occasion, they each wanted to be a part of the conversation with (god). And I discovered it simplified the process for me to assign each voice their own pen color as I wrote. It turns out that I had a strong feeling that there was only one appropriate color for each voice. Physical was brown, Emotional was pink, Mental

talking with (god)

(intellectual) was green, Spiritual was blue and my Ego was black. They all exhibited a distinct tone of voice, especially ego, and were easy to tell apart. This may seem very unusual and there is no doubt some might find this troubling, if not vaguely disturbing, psychologically speaking. Contrary to this possible opinion, I've come to believe it is wonderfully sane and extraordinarily healing. I guess if you've made it this far in the book, you're probably open to seeing where this goes before you decide. I hope so, because it could be life changing for you. It certainly has been for me.

Allowing each part of me to have their own voice has provided incredible insights that I believe could not have come from any other direction. One of the most powerful instances of this happened one day when my Spirit and Ego voices were at odds over something. The mild disagreement became a vehement argument, which totally shocked me, especially because I felt that my spiritual self would never engage in this way. And yet, it was, and not only that, but it wasn't giving an inch. It was a real stalemate until Lia stepped in. She was calm in her ethereal way. There was no confrontational energy at all, simply her pure presence. She asked both Spirit and Ego to sit back and take a rest. It felt like (god)'s version of a "time-out", where children are asked to sit in distant places to cool down. Lia then addressed Spirit and Ego, requesting that each of them think of something positive and genuine to say about the other, and that once they held that inside of themselves, to tell the other one what it was that they appreciated about them. Dead silence. For a long time. Finally, to my absolute surprise, Ego was the first to speak. Ego, in a calm, genuine voice told Spirit how valuable its contribution was to "our" life and how important it was that spirit pushed our boundaries, helping "us" to grow and expand in the world. Several moments went by in more silence. Apparently, Spirit was having a difficult time either coming up with what to say, or how to say it. Why? Why should that be so difficult?

talking with (god)

Eventually, Spirit spoke and complimented Ego for its valuable role in keeping us safe and protected. Spirit recognized that, by its very nature, it was always trying to expand into the universe somehow and that surely made ego's job very difficult because protection is its major purpose. After this exchange, things changed dramatically. There was far less friction inside of me. Not only that, but there was now a way to resolve inner conflicts, which had never existed before.

I am constantly amazed and filled with gratitude for all of my (god) relationships and for the precious insights and awarenesses brought about through my inner selves.

I'd like to share the essence of one of these conversations with you. I was wondering about how active Lia was in my life. What I meant was, did she do things *for* me, or did she just talk with me and then leave all of the actions up to me. My cultural history said it worked both ways, that (god) is responsible for everything (part of god's omnipotence) AND that we humans are responsible for everything (exercising our free will). How could it be both ways? How confusing for a mere human?

So, I asked Lia how it really worked. What she told me was so contrary to my training that it was difficult to grasp. Not that I didn't intellectually understand what she said, just that it was hard to believe and accept that she was open to the idea of me 'asking and testing her'. She said, "If you want to find out, ask me for things and test me and track the results." She told me, that despite what I've previously been taught by others, she was perfectly okay with this idea...more than okay actually, she *wanted* me to do it, so I could see for myself that it is her greatest desire to love me and be an active part of my life. This echoed what (god), in each voice, had previously told me, that (god) wants what I want, *or* something even better. This revelation flies in the face of everything I'd ever heard about (god). I'd heard that (god) has very specific expectations of each human being and that, in most cases, there would be some form of penalty or punishment for any failure to comply. And, here was (god) telling me that not only was this not true, but that (god) actually wanted what *I* wanted or something even better. I know that somehow, I was ready to hear this. I could appreciate that many others would not find this acceptable or believable. For me though, it was a wonderful statement which I found to be incredibly beautiful. And, in this conversation, Lia was telling me that it was her greatest desire to love me and be an active part of my life. *She told me to ask for anything, then test her and track the results.* Wow! Talk about being blown away.

So, what choice did I make? I started a journal in June of 2019 and wrote down everything I wanted, or at least all of the big things -- after all, I could probably handle the little stuff by myself. I added to the list constantly and kept track of the results, just as I'd been asked to do. In the first year, I recorded 122 requests, of which 113 happened. The remaining nine requests are pending. Part of me knows that the timing might not be right for receiving each of them yet *or* that there is "something even better in the works for me". I would have to say though, that this is an utterly convincing response to my question. Add to this, that the nature and scope of my requests was so broad and demanding that there was absolutely no way that *I* could ever have accomplished them all by myself. Not even close.

In many of my conversations, I would ask for an example to illustrate more practically what we were discussing and how it might apply to my life, so I thought I'd share one of my examples with you.

Maureen and I scheduled a trip in June 2019, first to San Francisco for three days and then on to the big island of Hawaii, for nine days. This would include ten to twelve hours of flight time plus layovers, which would give me plenty of time to read and digest a book by Michael Hyatt, titled *Platform*. This book explained everything I would need to do to effectively create and manage a website and blog. It promised to provide detailed information, so that every step of the way was covered. I researched Michael and discovered he was the real deal, who actually practiced what he preached. So, while still in the Albany, New York airport, I pulled out a brand-new notebook designed by my granddaughter, Kirsten and began taking notes. By the time we arrived in Hawaii, I'd covered all two hundred plus pages of his book and taken over 40 pages of detailed notes. I was feeling quite happy with my progress and plans were forming in my head based on what I'd written. Thank you, Michael!

The airplane we were on from San Francisco to Hawaii was gigantic and instead of the customary single seat pocket in front of me, there were two, so I placed Michael's book and Kirsten's adorable notebook in the upper pocket. When we landed, it was a bit chaotic, so I rushed in preparation for deplaning. We got off, went to the baggage claim area and picked up our suitcases, then jumped on the shuttle to the rental car location. Eventually, we got our car and drove a half hour north to our resort and checked in. A habit of mine is to unpack as soon as we arrive at our vacation destination so I can focus on feeling ready for fun, so that's what I did. We didn't have a ton of stuff, so within ten or fifteen minutes I was done. Hmmm, now where did I put the book and notebook? I searched. Nothing! I searched again and still nothing. I checked Maureen's stuff. Nothing. I threw a temper tantrum and actually stomped my foot, like an over tired two-year-old. Sad to admit, but I'm quite sure I swore a bit too. I mean really, all that diligent work, all those hours spent reading and all those notes, GONE!

Then, it dawned on me exactly where the book and notebook were. They were still on the airplane in the upper seatback pocket! Or, more likely the cleaning crew had thrown them out when getting ready for the return flight back to the mainland. There was a tiny, little bit of clarity of thought that popped into my mind. Hadn't Lia promised that I could ask her for anything and she would deliver? Yes, she had, I'd heard her with my own two ears. So, I decided that this would be an outstanding time to ask

talking with (god)

for her assistance. I sat down and tried to calm myself and release my angry adrenaline rush, so I could concentrate. And here's approximately what I said to her.

"Lia, please help me. I want to be able to go back to the airport, to the Lost and Found and have my notebook and Michael's book sitting there waiting for me. I trust you and believe in you and your promises to me, so please make this so. PS: By the way, I'm recording this in my journal, where I'm keeping all of my 'asks' of you and tracking the results, just like you asked me to. Thank you for your help."

We'd had an incredibly long day and I couldn't face going back to the airport right then. In two days, a friend of ours was coming to stay with us for the weekend and we'd need to pick him up from that same airport, so I decided I'd check at the 'lost and found' then. Pretty gutsy, huh? Part of me thought that waiting and not rushing back there would be a sign of good faith. Another part of me thought that part of me was crazy for waiting.

Two days later, we left for the airport early to give me some investigation time. We parked the car and I went to the United Airlines gate and spoke with one of the agents. She said that she couldn't directly help me, but that she would radio one of their support staff, who would come and talk with me. A few minutes later a woman, probably in her fifties, approached me and asked if she could help. I explained my dilemma and she asked me to follow her. We went around the corner of one of the buildings and came to a door. She got out her keys, opened the door and told me to go right in, which kind of surprised me, given all of the airport security we normally encounter. As we entered, she pointed to a very large bin, telling me that it was where all of their Lost and Found items were placed. There, sitting on the top of all of the items they'd collected, was my notebook, Michael's book and, as a bonus, the fiction book I'd also been reading! INCREDIBLE! Score number five for Lia, since this was the fifth

talking with (god)

"ask" I'd recorded in my journal. I'll tell you, this was a "eureka" moment for me.

Now that 112 more requests have been beautifully, freely given to me, I have come to rely on Lia, *knowing* what she is capable of providing for me. She has proven another of the things that (god) in all forms has told me, "Ask and know that you will receive and give thanks in advance of the receiving". The only times this has not been the case is when I know something even better is coming.

In case it might be of interest to you, I've included Appendix A, which gives some reasons why it is important to me to "speak my truth" and share with others what is important to me (which has led to this very book), and in Appendix B, I've listed some of the benefits I've experienced, as a result of my talking with (god).

talking with (god)

Opening the Door
(our story)

talking with (god)

The Beta Testers

Before we begin what, I have called "our story", because it is a collaboration between you, the reader, and me, I'd like to preface this section by acknowledging the invaluable contributions of a group of people I will refer to as, the "beta testers". Prior to writing this book, I asked a host of friends if they would like to take part in a project with me. I told them I was writing a book titled, _talking with (god)_, in which I would be sharing some of my experiences and providing instructions on how they could go about having their own conversations with (god). For those who agreed to participate, I explained a bit about my project, asked them to answer eight questions (see Appendix G), to read through some instructions about the process, and then to spend seven days having 15 to 20-minute conversations with (god) each day. Following their conversations, I requested they share some of their experiences with me. I told them I would love to hear all that they were comfortable sharing with me.

Forty-one people chose to participate in everything I asked. What I received was so deep and so rich, that I want to share much of it with you. So, as you read on, you'll see many quotes from them (which you can identify because they are in italics and you will see a person's initials in parentheses after the quotation), all of which provide keen insights and immensely broaden the scope and potential value of this book for you. What they've shared has widened my awareness and allowed me fuller vision into my life and my relationship with (god) and I am so grateful to them.

You can, of course, read this book in any order that you would like. That's up to you and your free will. But I do want to call your attention to some of the Appendices at the back of the book (in addition to the ones I have mentioned earlier). Appendices C through F summarize the answers to four of the questions I asked each of the beta-testers. You may find it interesting to see how a broad group of people describe themselves and their

talking with (god)

experiences during the beta testing. I have included this "data" with the idea that their backgrounds, challenges, and hopes may have some similarities with your own personal journey. In Appendix C you'll find their religious or spiritual backgrounds; in Appendix D, the names they use for (god); in Appendix E, a combined list of obstacles they anticipated or encountered during their conversations; and in Appendix F, a summary of the list of topics they wanted to talk with (god) about.

THE PROCESS

Now it's time to open the door for *you*.

I believe one essential ingredient in the process of talking with (god) is the practice of conceiving, believing and acting. To experience this powerful relationship, I believe it is necessary to be open to all possibilities (conceiving), to feel that the relationship and conversation will happen (believing) and then to take action, to make it a reality (acting). You're already taking one affirming step by reading this book. Please know that some doubts along the way are to be expected. Please feel free to express any doubts you encounter as a part of your dialogues with (god). Some of my most spectacular conversations have occurred because I expressed the doubts I was feeling. This book will have more to say about this, but for now just knowing doubts may happen is enough.

Whether you've been speaking with (god) for a long time or you're preparing for your first conversation, here's are my suggestions for your "practice", based on an approach that has worked for me.

talking with (god)

This is the BRIEF version of the process:

> Prepare
> Set your intention
> Choose the time and location
> Quiet yourself and breathe
> Ask and invite (god)
> Express gratitude, in advance
> Form a question or be open
> Listen from your heart
> Write what you hear and feel
> Recording results

At some point following your conversation, you may want to spend time reflecting on what you felt and discovered. In my practice, I've experienced very strong feelings and felt the need to write in a stream of consciousness, unfettered by intellectual and organizational concerns. I needed to be able to listen and speak directly from my heart and feelings. At other times, I've had specific practical questions and wanted advice I could follow to "fix" my problems or open my mind to new possibilities. I needed my mind fully engaged. There have even been instances where I've done both in one conversation or a string of conversations. Everything depends on your objective and is open for you to decide -- and, even to change your mind midstream and choose a new direction. My experience with (god), no matter which voice I hear or feel, is that (god) always goes the direction I want and will hear me out. Often, I've encountered startling and profound insights and needed to backtrack in the conversation, so I don't get lost. Anything you want or need to do will be okay with (god). It's all up to you to decide what feels "right" to you.

I'd like to expand on each of the steps in the process I use and share some wonderful and discerning quotes from the beta testers to show you how important it is to begin this process with a broad, wide-open mind and heart. I believe it will become

talking with (god)

apparent that there are many different approaches and that there is divine wisdom in choosing what feels "right" to you. This is all about you and your relationship with (god). What I provide is one approach that will give you a place to start, re-start or expand your conversational relationship. But, it is only *one* way. The quotes from the beta testers may encourage you to choose directions you might not otherwise have known or considered, had you read only *my* thoughts, so this book is richer because of them. I encourage you to read each one and see how they feel to you.

PREPARE

I believe we've all experienced times in our lives where we've questioned what we've been told. Occasionally, you may have found that the beliefs you grew up with no longer seem valid. Or, that they've shifted or become less stable. It's important in this process to be as honest as you can be. It's really the only way to have a sound, deep, interactive relationship. And, it matters that you are honest with (god) and honest with yourself.

> *"I still hesitate to say I'm talking to god because I was never comfortable with the God that I was brought up to know in the Catholic church. I felt much more comfortable thinking of this as my higher self or inner voice. Thinking of it as a part of me helped me to feel comfortable and more receptive to the messages- who knows me and my issues better than me!"* (EM)

As you prepare, it is also important to realize that there are many ways to create a conversational relationship. One way is to mirror someone else's process (perhaps in this case, mine), and this approach can be extraordinarily helpful at the start. But then, if you feel drawn or led in another direction, you may be concerned that you are doing it "wrong". It's wonderful to keep in mind that there is no *right or wrong way,* and that there is

talking with (god)

enormous value in being open to what happens and not overly invested in a specific set of steps or outcome.

> *"Probably the most important part of the whole process is making it your own. Each day/conversation is going to be a little different. We can't expect to always hear a clear voice or be taken to new depths. Some days, we will just be quiet, hear our pulse getting in sync with (god)'s and that's what our time that day is meant to be. We are simply there, totally present in our intent to be open -- whatever does or doesn't happen that might be new, revelatory or unexpected. So, I guess what this means is that we shouldn't get too caught up in our intent."* (MM)

Sometimes you may begin a conversation and have a strong need for it to solve a problem or provide an answer. At times, this may make it more challenging because your need is pressing. Yet, even in this circumstance, it can be very freeing to remain open to what happens, knowing anything is possible with (god).

> *"Obvious, perhaps, but each day will be different and trying to force God's manifestation or my response to be the same is counterproductive".* (MM)

It can also be very helpful as you prepare for conversations to open your heart and mind, see what comes into your consciousness and "plant a seed", allowing it to germinate.

> *"My "practice" for talking to (god) evolved. I began with the intention of a specific time, place and rituals. However, I found that the best way for me was to plant a seed and listen for answers. I plant my seeds prior to sleeping, while creating art, or walking in nature and let the voices or messages come".* (SR)

talking with (god)

SET YOUR INTENTIONS

It's very helpful to begin by <u>setting an intention</u> of openness and giving yourself the freedom to speak from your heart and to hear (god's) voice from within. As it turns out, there is a significant difference between intention and expectation. "Intentions" are general courses of action, while "expectations" are specific desired outcomes.

> *"I feel that intention is very important and that it is important to realize the difference between intention and expectation. It might be a very wise thing to set a clear intention, and not have any expectations. Don't expect to hear a voice or have visions right off the bat (and this may never happen). The answer may come through as a distracting thought that pulls you to look at your bookshelf that takes you to a passage in a book with the answer that you needed. This has happened to me a lot, I was not experienced enough with meditation to "hear" the answers. I would throw my concern out to the universe and say "show me". I often found myself at the library just walking down the aisle and a book would catch my eye. Sometimes I would get it home and read a few paragraphs and a light bulb would go off. Then it seemed I would lose interest in it. I didn't force myself to read on, as usually I had gotten what I was looking for in those few paragraphs. I also started to get inspiration for art projects and to call friends that I hadn't talked to in a while. Sometimes the answer would be in a Facebook post, or a side conversation I would have later that day. The more I followed these inklings of interests, the more I would find glimpses of joy and one serendipitous event after another."* (EM)

I recall one enlightening conversation I had with Lia where I asked for a very specific outcome. She let me talk until I had exhausted myself and then pointed out that, while she loved

talking with (god)

hearing all that I had to say, she wondered if I understood that by setting my heart on only one acceptable outcome, that I was limiting her ability to help me. She told me that she always respects my free will, and then reminded me that she wants what I want or something even better. My limiting her to one acceptable outcome would prevent her from assisting in providing the "something even better". When I heard this, I was blown away. Of course, it made sense, but I was too focused and single-minded to see that I was creating confining limits. And really, what made me think that I could know all of what was available to me and choose wisely what was best, as Lia could? Shifting from expectations to intentions has made my life easier and given (god) freedom and room to maneuver and be more involved in my life.

CHOOSE TIME and LOCATION

If you are beginning your journey, here are a few suggestions about choosing a time and a location, that may help open your conversational relationship. If you're already experienced, you probably have an established routine that works for you, and yet you may pick up some new ideas as well.

The best time is the one that fits your schedule. That may sound obvious and simplistic, but often when folks are given instructions to follow, they might believe the process won't work unless they comply. I believe that flexibility is very important. I suggest starting by choosing a time where you can spend 15 to 20 uninterrupted minutes. If you can stay with this time each day, if your schedule allows, it may be easier than trying to fit it in around other things. Given my experience and that of others I've spoken to, it can be any time of day, so long as it works for you. Sometimes, you'll have strong intentions of maintaining a schedule, and that will work well for you. Other times, you may have to adjust your plan and be flexible. Being open has its advantages and offers freedom for your practice.

talking with (god)

> *"I found that you cannot do this on a schedule; it happens when it happens."* (RB)

> *"When the time is right for your conversation to take place, find a quiet and comfortable place you can go to, to be at peace with yourself so as to listen to sound or feeling you get. No matter what day, time or otherwise it might be, do what is needed for yourself. This conversation is between you and (god) and no one else. Be specific."* (DM)

It also happens that you may not be able to set aside time as you would prefer. It's important to know that you can communicate with (god) wherever you are and whenever you get the chance.

> *"I also got the leading that it wasn't necessary to sit somewhere separate; that it was okay to ask questions or talk to God as I went about the mundane tasks of daily living."* (CM)

Some conversations you may want to spend writing, meditating or in some other relaxing way. It's a great idea to try different methods to see what works best for you and be open to (god). This is important for choosing a time and a location.

> *"First, I would meditate for 10-20 minutes and ask questions. But, my Voice (capitalized means my 'sacred' voice) said: "Be still, slow down, too many questions, let go of doing for others…". So instead I went for long walks on a straight open path where I have experienced conversations with Spirit for years."* (EG)

Whatever you decide, I recommend always having a notebook, journal or pad and pen or pencil handy, so you can write down anything you wish to keep and review later. I've done this the whole time I've been talking with (god) and have profited

talking with (god)

immensely from being able to read my conversational notes later.

QUIET YOURSELF and BREATHE

Since everyone may have their own method of moving into stillness, please feel free to do what quiets you the most, perhaps closing your eyes and gently breathing in and out. Sometimes playing soothing instrumental background music can be very helpful and set the mood for a relaxed, but attentive state of mind.

Part of the aim here is to release your attachments to mental thoughts and set the stage for having a conversation with (god). Resting in silence can be a wonderful lead in.

> *"I've come to realize that I prefer being in the silence when possible. I feel more in the moment and more able to listen."* (PK)

> *"(I find) you must be silent and alert to the sensation of the quietness you are feeling while you are alone. Be aware of sounds the moment in time you are listening for. To speak to (god) is absolutely a positive vibration your ears will hear (or) maybe as a feeling you get through your nerve endings."* (DM)

And encountering a sense of harmony and peace also contributes greatly.

> *"The best part of having a conversation is the feeling of peace when I talk with him. I also find that God is always with me, good or bad. I know one thing that is for sure, when I talk to Him, I feel inner peace and calmness".* (AL)

My practice centers around writing. Most often, I sit at my desk, quiet my mind, open my notebook and away I go. The majority of

talking with (god)

time, I begin the conversation and (god) enters in when I'm done writing. This isn't exclusively the case. Sometimes, I need to be on the move or doing something that occupies my mind and then when my rhythm shifts to a slower pace, I can talk to (god) and actually hear what (god) has to say.

One of the most fascinating things about asking for input from the beta testers was the wide range of ways in which they connected to (god). Let me share some of them with you, in hopes that you find ones that feel appealing to you or to use as an alternative to your standard practice. The ones mentioned were:

talking with (god)

Artwork- It didn't seem to matter what form it took, as long as it engaged the individual's creative side. Interestingly, it also wasn't necessary that the artwork appear professional. What did matter was that it reflected something personally meaningful.

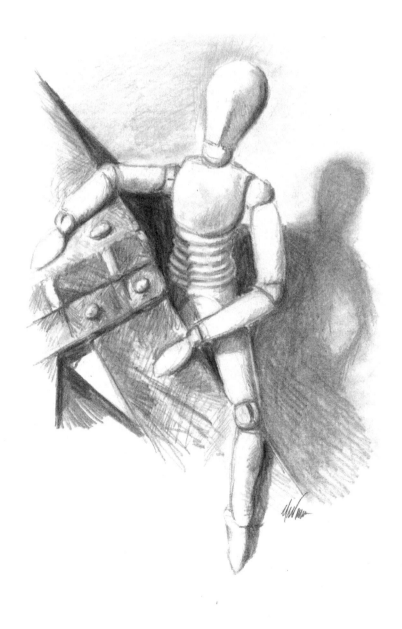

talking with (god)

Music- Sometimes conversations were begun as a result of the individual's personal musical expression. Other times listening to some form of soothing music set the stage for peace, relaxation and then an unfolding conversation.

talking with (god)

Walking-Often the act of walking, especially with no destination in mind, helped open things up and create space for a dialogue.

talking with (god)

Swimming-Surprisingly, the act of swimming can clear the mind and release the constant stream of thoughts that sometimes stand in the way of a conversation.

talking with (god)

Breathing- One of the most helpful practices is the simple focus on one's breathing. There are many techniques and ways to ease into different breathing patterns, but all of them seem to create a marvelous space for having a dialogue.

talking with (god)

Meditating- There are many ways to meditate and numerous books that can help anyone come into a beautiful meditative state. No matter how one chooses to meditate, it is a fabulous way to become peaceful and receptive to whatever conversation you wish to have.

talking with (god)

Mantras- Creating a mantra of your own or using mantras which have been around for over a thousand years, they can be wonderful ways to tune into your inner world and begin a conversation from a place a calmness.

talking with (god)

Prayer- Whether written, spoken, sung or chanted, all forms of prayer have the power to shift one's state of being, opening the door for a blessed conversation.

talking with (god)

Poetry- When the words and feelings are personal and connective, whether they come from reading someone else's poetry or writing your own, the stage can be set for a wonderful dialogue.

talking with (god)

Reading- There are so many excellent books and stories available to read and gain inspiration from, probably right on your own bookshelf. Anything that creates an opening or a deeper awareness can assist in beginning a conversation.

talking with (god)

Yoga- Devotees of the practice of yoga, as well as those new to the experience, know how incredibly valuable yoga is as both exercise and meditation. It opens and creates a beautiful space inside, making it a sensational way to initiate a dialogue.

talking with (god)

Writing- This activity, which you probably guessed by now is my favorite, allows me to interact directly because I write what is in me and then what I receive in response from (god). I like the tactile experience of using a pen or pencil and paper, but other means, like a computer work for many people. It doesn't matter what method you choose; it only matters that it provides you a way of opening your heart.

All of these practices helped them create and deepen their connection to (god) opening the path for valuable conversations.

talking with (god)

ASK and INVITE (god)

In your heart and mind, ask for an awareness of (god's) presence inside you and invite (god) to speak with you.

How (god) appears to you may be very different from the way (god) appears to others. There are truly many paths and many views. I encourage you to choose whatever feels most right to you, even if it doesn't coincide with what others believe.

> *"God for me is a silent, vibrational field; a constant companion, and in the most precious "form" for me – a Living Love, timeless and all kind and powerful."* (WH)

And once you have decided to ask (god) to be with you, inviting (god)'s presence into your mind and heart, go "all in", allowing anything and everything to come into your consciousness.

> *"Once I have dropped into that field of love I start writing down my questions for God and then writing down His responses. Asking and receiving as my pen flows over the pages."* (JH)

I invite you to give yourself permission to be open for the answers that (god) wants to share with you.

> *"I asked (god) for help seeing myself as a beloved daughter. I learned, "That is how I see you all. You are that." And when I asked if (god) felt a longing to be seen, heard and loved. I was told:' "Funny question. I don't see it that way. I am love. Love I am. And in ways your words cannot express." The messages I got were loving."* (HD)

What you hear may surprise you. You may find that you knew far more than you thought you did. Try, as best you can, to be open to that also.

talking with (god)

> *"What I noticed when I would ask a question and get quiet, was that some of my messages which I may have known in my mind, but it felt like it was more powerful and coming from the heart."* (DA)

Sometimes you may find that there are delays between your question and your answer. This is probably inevitable. One explanation for this may be what (god) told me. (god) said that if I allowed an openness in my mind and heart, it provided (god) with flexibility to answer when "the time was right for it to benefit me the most". This can be extraordinarily challenging, depending on the nature of the question and the need for an answer. When I am able to give (god) this "space", I find the answers far more satisfying. I also find that I become more comfortable waiting, because my experiences have reassured me that (god) always wants the best for me. So, it becomes very much an issue of trust, and this can take time to build. The only way to know for sure about this process is to give it a try and see what happens.

> *"Every time I wrote, I got something. Even on the night when it was too late. And I had a prayer answered by the next morning."* (HD)

EXPRESS YOUR GRATITUDE, IN ADVANCE

Express your gratitude, in advance, for your conversation with (god). I added this element very late in my process, having misunderstood the concept for much of my life.

I did understand the idea of gratitude and appreciation. Like most children, I was coached from an early age to say "thank you" whenever I received a gift. I also learned it was often either expected or demanded, which didn't feel right to me at all. Perhaps that's why it became confusing for me. What if I didn't like what I was given, did I still have to say 'thank you'? Yes, I did. But, why? The answer to this question was, "because that's what people do". I wondered, "So, how can you tell the difference between when a person is genuinely thankful and when they are just abiding by others expectations?" The answer to this seems to be, you can't.

The second part of this statement encourages you to be grateful, *in advance*. This was the part that troubled me most. How can you know for sure that you are going to receive what you ask for? Isn't it presumptuous to always expect a "yes" answer? Wouldn't it be wiser to wait and see whether you are happy with the answer and then express your gratitude? I know logic supports this idea, but from my experience, (god) doesn't operate according to human logical standards. What I discovered was that my statement of faith and trust that (god) loved me and would provide for me in all situations *was* the core issue. (God) reminded me, that (god) wants what I want or something even better. (God) asked me to be trusting and to know that I would receive the best, most beautiful answer, even if it wasn't the one I had in mind. I eventually came to understand that, *expressing gratitude, in advance*, was an affirmative statement on my part, proclaiming my belief in (god's) love and care for me. This action on my part removed all obstacles in (god)'s way and lifted my heart from any inner resistance, making it possible for me be open, accepting and grateful.

> *"I am so grateful for this time to truly talk with God about what is really important; relationships, honesty, passion, love and authenticity. The frenetic must do's and must haves aren't real."* (DA)

I also found that (god) has a sense of humor. One time I was expressing my gratitude and excitement for all that (god) was sharing with me. I said, "Thank you so, so much!" -- to which (god) responded, "You are most welcome. I am excited as well." This surprised me, so I said to (god), "Really, you get excited?" (God) answered, "Of course, who do you think invented excitement?"

talking with (god)

FORM A QUESTION or BE OPEN

Depending on your intention you may want to bring to mind a *question* or concern you'd like to talk about or you may want to be completely *open*, without any specific expectations.

It may be helpful to think of this time as a blank slate, which you can fill with anything. In my conversations, nothing is ever off the table and trust me, I have a lot of questions! I haven't run out of them yet and I believe that (god) is happy about this, because (god) tells me so. And (god) reassures me and 'sees' me.

> *"Spirit (god): No other person has ever been YOU going through the exact situation YOU are going through in this moment in time. You hold all the answers you seek. Now you are thinking, "If I knew the answer I wouldn't be asking the question." You as a physical entity, may not intellectually "know" the answer, but I do and I live within you. I am a part of you as you are a part of me. I know all and am all. Why would you go to any other place for the answer? You have ALL answers through me. You think you need answers but really what you need is faith."* (EM)

I believe that (god) wants to spend time with each of us and share in our lives. (God) wants us to know that it is (god's) pleasure to listen to us.

> *"When I spoke to God there was always an answer but not always one that was easy to follow up on, especially, I noticed, when it came to setting boundaries. Boundaries that were needed for my emotional growth. I gained insight in how I may be contributing to a problem and what needs to be done to find peace and acceptance. I know that God is forever present in me and has been a guidance in my life even when I was not aware, or present in God."* (AB)

It seems to me, after all of my conversations, that (god) loves to be involved with us and offer guidance, if we ask for it. And

talking with (god)

sometimes, (god) sees the wisdom in inviting us to answer our own questions.

> *"The guidance I received did help me each time: I thought it was interesting to get a question as an answer to my own request. It was in my opinion, an invitation to learn how to find my own answers."* (MP)

I've discovered that conversations can travel in many directions, sometimes even within the same conversation. There are also times too when I don't feel the impact of the conversation right away. It kind of sneaks up on me and surprises me.

> *"I would write a question or present a situation but not be able to connect right then. But over time, being open, something would happen to trigger the response. Since this started, I had eight complete conversations. A couple so profound, that when I go back and reread, it's surprising that it came out of me.... but maybe through me instead."* (RB)

At times, my mind would get ahead of me and my pen could not keep up. Insights would form and blossom in my mind and I couldn't always catch them in time to write them down. When this happened, I asked (god) to slow down, knowing that (god) knew every answer to every question I had (or ever would have, I believed).

> *"I have had some good insights through this process and I really feel like there's a Voice there that's poised with the answer before I asked the question."* (JF)

LISTEN with YOUR HEART

In this sacred, loving space, *listen from your heart* for (god's) voice, being open to all possibilities. Rest in this beautiful space you've created.

55

talking with (god)

Since anything is possible with (god), you never know what to expect.

> *"I went into this experience with an open mind not trying to project an outcome. Did I have a dialog with God - no. Did I hear a word or words that were not mine – yes. Did I experience God's presence - definitely yes. I felt great calmness and deep peace."* (DF)

You may ask for anything and when you are quiet and your heart is open, you may also receive anything.

> *"I talked to God about my desire to be comfortable enough financially to feel that I can donate. The response was to do it from a giving heart, not a feeling of duty or obligation, in gratitude for what's provided. Not with anxiety, as anxiety comes from fear. Shortly thereafter, I received funds I wasn't expecting."* (CM)

Allowing your heart to be open provides space for whatever you most need at the time.

> *"The moments I truly relaxed and opened my heart, I felt such peace. I heard answers that were so comforting and full of love. On these nights, I drifted back into such a peaceful sleep and woke up with joy. The answers to my questions were in my heart (like they were there all of the time)."* (EG)

My mood is not always the same during my talks with (god). Sometimes there is an emotional overtone. (God, in this case, Lia) told me it's okay to scream, cry, be angry, upset or any other emotion and once I'm done with that, I can make a new choice. I am not bound to ANY single choice I've made or to any feeling I've felt. There is great freedom in this and I know that (god) can read me and will sit with me and listen to me. And (god) will also respond to me.

talking with (god)

> *"Spirit (god): You are not alone in this. You are surrounded by love. It is always scary to do the next right thing. If you let fear guide your path, you will stay where you are. You will not move forward. Have faith and embrace the love that is in you and around you. You are uncomfortable with loving yourself. Once you believe your own worth, you will not hesitate to take care of your needs. Once you lovingly care for yourself, you will see how easy it is to care for others in a genuine way. It will not take such an effort."* (EM)

It is interesting to me that (god) does not demonstrate any need to provide intellectual answers, unless that's what I've directly asked for. Often (god) speaks in images or uses simple words to convey messages.

> *"Almost all of my "messages" come in very brief and simple terms. Not flowery. Literally, everything I wrote under "receive" was what came when being quiet and listening...they did not feel like thoughts at all.... but things received. I just wrote them down as they came. I had intentions for the day but didn't really have questions, per se. I just knew that whatever came, I needed to hear."* (DL)

Sometimes the message is repetitive, which can be a real blessing, and through the simplicity we can remain focused.

> *"Listen from your HEART! Learn from your HEART! Respond to your HEART! I've come to accept that TALKING WITH GOD will help me exercise my HEART more frequently."* (JT)

At other times we want to hear (god)'s precious voice, one that we'll recognize. It's one thing for someone else to tell us of their experiences, but when we feel it ourselves, it's quite another.

talking with (god)

> *"If only I could hear from (god). That would be the most precious voice my ears could hear. Others say they have communicated with (god)-- but the belief is in the hearing, not being told by others. My heart and ears are open and willing to listen, with all intent for answers I'm looking for."* (DM)

> *"It's hard to explain exactly the tone of voice I'm hearing. It's more like a feeling from my heart. I'm still getting to know (god) so, sometimes it's hard knowing what I'm hearing. If only I could hear a voice that would come across as a voice that speaks to my ears so they would immediately alert me so generously and preciously to my heart. I believe my tears would flow like a stream unleashed from heaven above, to pick up my feelings and crush all other sounds around me."* (DM)

(God) has a wonderful way of bringing clarity to us. At times, confusing questions may form in our minds. We may wonder about the voice we hear and who it belongs to and we may need some advice from our heart.

> *"Clarification about whether we are talking with (god)...)-- Is this our higher self, or us, as (god) beings, or what? If we are wondering and want a way to tell if we are speaking with (god), we could ask ourselves; is it a kind and loving voice? If it is, then we probably are, but if it is a judgmental or angry voice, it is probably our ego speaking."* (GH)

Sometimes we need to remember who we are and what makes us special. What role does love play in our lives? (God), in my experience, is very happy to remind us and encourage us to practice love for ourselves. When this happens, I find my heart grows several sizes and I tend to shine.

talking with (god)

At times I believe (god)'s voice comes through our spiritual self, but the words are meant for our earth self and we're encouraged to show great care and love.

> *"(god speaking): To connect with the radiant self, appreciate yourself. Where are you appreciating your life? The two times you consciously connected with your magnificent Self, you were loving yourself, you were tender and appreciatively. It is simple, if you get it. The way is to LOVE YOU, your life, your expression. Your life is your love song. What is your song? Are you singing love or are you singing something else? Find that love, my child. Love (her). She is magnificent. Remember. Shower her with your attention. Take care of her. She is the one you need to love and appreciate. You were given her in your care. This is the one you MUST take care of. The rest falls from the relationship with her. What thoughts are you feeding her? What joys are you feeding her? What experiences are you feeding her? This is the key for you. LOVE her. Love (her). This is what was shown to you back then. LOVE is the key."* (KR)

WRITE WHAT YOU HEAR and FEEL

If/when a conversation develops, you may want to open your eyes, grab your notebook/journal and pen and *write down what you hear and feel*, both *your* words and those of (god). Or, you may want to stay in the moment until your conversation is complete and then write down what you experienced.

I want to take a minute here to say something VERY IMPORTANT. When I use the word, "conversation", what I mean is a "connection" you experience with (god). The connection may very well be a conversation, but it may be something else. It may be a set of images or feelings. It may be a sense of inner guidance or knowing, with no words attached. My connections are almost always through words, but this fact is not meant to

59

talking with (god)

suggest that this is the *right way* or the *only way*, it's just *my way*. As you can see from reading some of the beta testers experiences that follow, there are many ways to be connected to (god).

Often, searching for guidance, is what is hoped for.

> *"Guidance came in an overwhelming feeling within me, no words but more of a release that allowed me to know what I needed to do. I guess like clearing a block of energy within that needed to be freed." (AB)*

> *"(Speaking about (god)…) I'm not entirely sure "who" this source is. It answers to whatever I call it and has never confirmed exactly what or who, but I don't really care anymore. I think the point is that it has offered me divine guidance and counsel, which is exactly what I've been seeking. In this process I have certainly been able to have faith in the greater purpose and divine will. I have come around to the idea that this force is god, but not as was defined by my upbringing. I've found, the best part of this journaling practice is that it has helped me define my spirituality in my own terms. The guidance I receive does not come from any church or religion -- it's my own spiritual practice and the teachings I receive always feel unarguably and authentically true". (EM)*

At other times, there is a strong need to hear (god)'s voice. Sometimes this happens and sometimes it's not a voice, but thoughts that offer direction or insight.

> *"Although the internal voice I was hearing was mine, I believe it was actually God directing my thoughts in the direction he wanting me to go. It was a kind voice that lifted my spirits and placed me in the position to succeed and to live a fulfilling life. The voice I typically listen to is a loud and overpowering one that tells me I'm not good enough or*

that I can't do that. It's so strong that I don't even notice the soft spoken one telling me to listen deep within and yes, that I am worthy and yes, God does want me to succeed." (MW)

"In regards to my experience: if I am just sitting and "listening" I don't actually "hear" anything. Maybe some people hear a voice, but I don't. What I receive seems just to be thoughts. I would say these "thoughts" were always there but I wasn't registering that they were part of an ongoing conversation with god. Somehow picking up a pen and paper and dividing those thoughts into Q & A format helped me see that they were not entirely my own thoughts. After that, it took some faith and talking to others to really believe in the process. I think that faith and intention are the two big players in talking to god." (EM)

"I discovered the power of letting the messages come through drawing or painting. (MM) ----

talking with (god)

"If we are gifted with sight, we spend a great deal of our life viewing the world. We experience a free flow of images and create a host of our own. They form a different kind of language and are capable of speaking to us in unique ways. When this happens, we often need no words at all. We feel whole and content. And, many times, underneath the images we see, are the answer we seek." (MM)

talking with (god)

"Another conversation also led me to move from written words to a picture. This time, (god) directed me to the world around me to hear his voice. I was caught up in watching an orchid on a tree outside my window, which was on a very slender stem with only two blossoms being blown by the wind. It seemed so vulnerable, yet was held very strongly by the many roots that wrapped the tree. The word that came to me was "resilience." I felt I had to draw this, and then I began seeing/feeling this idea of being surrounded, protected and kept safe by roots. I could feel that the roots somehow were also nourishing me. What I wrote in my journal was: "God, you hold me so securely that I can radiate your calm, peace, and joy -- and I can send it out to people around me." My first sketch led me to another, more finished, drawing and painting that reminds me that I am surrounded by (god)'s love." (MM)

talking with (god)

"While "experimenting," with a deeper listening practice, I discovered the power of letting the messages from (god) come through drawing or painting. Based on the story of the disciples walking with Jesus on the way to Emmaus, I was focusing on the idea of "Stay with us/me." From meditating on this, I was guided to create a little paint sketch of what it is like when I allow (god) to walk with me, to be in me and radiating out from me. The illustration here is a slightly refined version of my first sketch. Creating the original as an expression of what (god) was helping me to experience <u>in that moment</u> about (their) presence within me. Making the first sketch, and drawing and painting the second version, gave me such a lot of joy – a joy I feel each time I look at it." (MM)

"My sense of God's presence was for the most part an inner voice and a very warm soft positive feeling. It changed once in a while. For example, once I was lying in the grass and our conversation was punctuated by a ray of sunshine that hit my chest and meant "YES", or the sound of a bird nearby that meant "NO". (MP)

"What struck me was that usually there was a blend of very ordinary stuff with answering a question I didn't ask or wasn't even thinking about. Also, I had several images that just arrived; usually it was an image that spoke to me. " (DL)

"First thing that came were images: an animal, a river, and I drew the symbol that popped up. God asked me to look into the meaning of my latest project: making dreamcatchers for people. He helped me understand the deeper meaning underneath the project." (MP)

talking with (god)

> *"I felt the Spirit around me and a sense of being lifted up. On the other two days I found myself lifting my arms up, not flying like a bird but being lifted closer to God."* (MM)

Some of the most spectacular connections I've had have come through the feelings I experienced. There can be such an intimacy inside of these connections and such warmth and tenderness.

> *"I expected to have a physical feeling of some kind when I prayed - something that would let me know He was there. I wanted confirmation that not only was He with me, but that he was supporting me, or maybe that I was doing what he wanted me to do. I'm not sure that ever came, but what I do know is that when I was writing, sketching and painting, it felt like God was in the message. Our communication was intimate. It was personal to my life with Him. It was wrought with pain and lessons learned. It was also filled with amazing earthly Angels, who lifted me up when I didn't have the energy. That's where God lived. He lived in the beautiful souls here on earth, managing this chaos along with me, and you know what? Sometimes I was that angel, offering support to others, maybe even like this message to you, or in your asking me to help you write a book about communicating with God."* (MD)

> *"I can't seem to focus. I'm assuming it's from our current situation. (COVID19 PANDEMIC) What I did experience was feelings of warmth and being surrounded by love and I did have some visions of my guides and angels."* (KS)

> *"My conversations with God/Goddess have been tender and powerful. (I received) a poem from my beloved late husband that came through, (which was) a great gift to me."* (VW)

talking with (god)

It is both fascinating and rewarding to be open to whatever the connection with (god) may bring to you. Having an intention to be present offers you freedom to experience anything.

> *"(And what I heard (god) say was) … be present to what is within you … for the answers to all questions are in your feelings … use these feelings to direct you to move into areas of unparalleled bliss."* (BT)

> *"(God) speaks to me in songs and music".* (SB)

> *"One of the things that surprised me is the exactness of the words that I wrote. Thoughts arise faster than my pen writes. But, just as I am about to write a word, another word appears for me to write, and it is a perfect expression of the message that I am writing."* (PF)

IF NOTHING HAPPENS (OPTIONS)

If nothing happens right away, enjoy the quiet and continue, remaining open.

If still nothing comes, there are three additional thoughts I suggest.

The first is to accept that no conversation occurred, then to offer yourself and (god) love, knowing that you can try again and write down anything you did experience.

The second option is the same as the first, except that you may want to write down and take notice of any obstacles or challenges you experienced with calming your mind. I've had this happen many times and at the end of this book you can read Appendix (H), which will assist you with "ways through the noise", which may prove helpful for you.

talking with (god)

A third option if you are not hearing (god)'s voice or experiencing any connection, is to continue enjoying the quiet, offer yourself and (god) love and *imagine* what (god) would have said to you or shared in images or feelings, then write down what you imagined you would have experienced. This may seem strange, but I've noticed that this method releases my thoughts and expectations, creating a greater opening for me to then hear what (god) actually has to share. It has also been true that what I *imagined* (god) sharing was incredibly helpful to me.

It's also very important to realize that you might not be ready for a particular conversation or to hear answers to your questions. (God) always respects your free will and waits until you are truly ready. Although it may be disappointing if this happens, I've discovered that accepting it, offering love to myself and (god), and knowing I can try again, serves me best.

At times, we downplay anything other than what we ideally want to happen, not realizing that what actually did happen was perfect for us at the time. Experiencing relaxation is in itself a wonderful thing and may be exactly what we needed most.

> *"(I found that I experienced) no specific communication result as to answers, guidance, talking, etc., (however I) enjoyed the exercise, and certainly the ability to get back to something that provides a meditative and relaxing state at least once a day."* (MS)

IF YOU ENCOUNTER OBSTACLES

There are probably an unlimited number of obstacles that could interfere with you connecting with (god). In Appendix E, the beta testers identified well over 50 different obstacles they anticipated encountering. They can take any form and enter the conversation at any time. It's important to know that you can release any obstacle and that (god) will help you.

talking with (god)

Sometimes, it's the simple distractions of life.

> *"One of the biggest challenges to my conversations is distractions. Every day things pop in your head, cooking, chores etc. You have to constantly get back on track. In my daily conversations with God I have come to realize a number of things about myself and I seem to feel closer to God when I am in a small group or by myself as opposed to a crowded church. This exercise has helped me experience a closer relationship with God which I will continue to work on and try to improve."* (KL)

Other times, in our openness, we are filled with emotions which overtake us; self-judgment, shame, anger, sadness and fear. (God) knows all of these emotions and will listen carefully, both to what you say and to how you feel. (God) is never any of these things. God is only love and accepts us in whatever way we approach, always listening and offering support.

> *"(Asking for advice, I was told) ... First stop comparing yourself to other people ... as you are judging yourself ... and that is limiting you from flourishing ... trust and let go ... as you let go ... listen to inspiration, intuition and take action on that."* (BT)

> *"Spirit (god): Shame comes from the false belief that you are unworthy of love. It is a deceptive illusion, as is fear. You are worthy of love because you are light created of love. As for your ideal of living a life of love and conquering fear -- this is an ideal, a concept. This goes back to the original topic of knowledge versus wisdom. You "know" what to do, but now is your chance to practice it. Every moment presents a choice. You can choose love or fear. If you miss this opportunity to choose love, just blink and you will have another one. Don't condemn yourself for the times that you choose fear. Have faith. I am here to guide you. You are not alone. If you keep your eyes open and*

stick with me, I will show you how one of faith can become "wise beyond her years." Wasn't that the point of your question tonight? You wanted to know how to speed up the learning curve?" (EM)

The one obstacle unfortunately is need of more faith and how to talk to (god)...prayer doesn't always give the answer we're looking for." (DM)

"On the very first day, my intent was to let go of anger, stress, and be cleansed. I was blessed by the vision and sense of a waterfall all around me. It was big and powerful, but where I was standing it was gentle. At one point I heard my name being called. I felt like I could stay there as long as I wanted and I could/can go back there any time I want. I felt "detoxed," calm, and I lost track of time." (MM)

"I also saw in my journaling that I started to put a voice to my feelings. I feel sad and have had years of feeling disconnected and sad, then I found myself being guided to put a voice to the sadness. Sadness would say joy was over rated and keeping status quo was ok. When I wrote that, I laughed. Here I have been trying to feel more joy and it wasn't until I leaned into the sadness and grief, to give it a name, did I realize it had kept me safe on some level. I can now choose differently and to let go and be more open for joy and passion and love. The next day I continued and this time my conversation was with joy, it started with gratitude for lightness, honestly and freedom." (DA)

"I found myself filled with fear, afraid that I would fail and would not experience anything. I wept with that fear, I wept about all the things I let distract my attention from (god), and I asked for help and boom, whether it was imagined or not doesn't matter to me. I was told, "You are a beloved daughter of the universe". (HD)

talking with (god)

"In my conversations with God I was able to share my fears and listen for guidance. Often times it was to do one thing to stay in action and to value myself first. I know this in my head, but this has been a shift to really feel and know that I am Divinely guided, protected, and loved." (DA)

(God) is aware that we aren't always comfortable with our own interpretations about our life and the events we experience. I believe (god) knows we are often confused about our own story and why we are here.

"Spirit (god): When one measures things using linear time, you are likely to assign them periods, chapters, beginnings, middles, ends, or a number of other temporal terms. This doesn't translate to where I am. Here there is no time. Experiences mix together. You don't lose sight of something that happened "a long time ago" because everything is occurring simultaneously. In this way, you have all experiences to guide your progress forward with less likelihood of repeating lessons learned. You see, the problem with "closing a chapter" of your life is that you are apt to lock up the details of the lessons learned during that period and quickly forget them. This is why people tend to repeat old behavior patterns and make the same "mistakes" over again. (I use this word because it is how you think of these events. Really it is a learning opportunity.) If the lesson repeats, I would say you haven't learned it completely. You can increase your learning curve by keeping fresh in your mind the lessons you've learned this year and review them often so as not to repeat them as time passes and memories fade." (EM)

I think (god) realizes we need help with all of our forms of communication, words, thoughts, feelings, everything.

talking with (god)

> *"An obstacle I encountered was the notion that I was to talk to and hear, in words, from Spirit. While waiting for the words, I was rather dismissive of the subtler feelings that permeated my being and nonetheless provided loving nudges and sometimes clear cut albeit wordless direction. Going forward I will be more accepting of the many ways that I experience communication from Source....seeing, hearing, feeling and a deep, profound knowing that defies language. It was richly sensual and showed up in many ways, my relatively concrete expectations notwithstanding." (DS)*

> *"My primary concern is how can I live out my passions and still make a living. Trust and faith are major stumbling blocks for me. I know what drives me- I've been able to come to an understanding of myself to that extent. I haven't been able to figure out how to get there." (JS)*

RECORDING RESULTS

This is a sacred process and hopefully it will provide you with a deepening relationship with (god), in whatever way feels most right to you. Your connection with (god) may be profound, offering you insights, guidance, wellness or inner wisdom or it may simply be a perfectly peaceful place for you to rest and separate yourself from everything else for a while. The world can be extremely challenging and we can easily be thrown off balance. We may need help regaining our health, wellness or sense of peace and turn to (god) for assistance.

> *"This experience has taught me to quiet my mind for a few minutes each day and talk with God. Due to everything happening right now <COVID19 pandemic>. I was so anxious, that my blood pressure was sky high. I quieted my mind, and felt God's peace, telling me we would be OK. After about two days, my blood pressure returned to*

> *normal, and has remained so ever since. I am going to continue with this project, and hope to get better at it. I feel I have a good relationship with God, and my challenges are to quiet my mind."* (MET)

> *"I wrote that I felt a peaceful, warm spirit presence in me. And two things came to me – to be generous and to be grateful. I felt peaceful and loving, and it really made a difference in my day."* (PK)

If we consider our strengths and talents, we know we have an incredible ability to aid in our own process of development. Believing in ourselves isn't always easy. Some of us have been taught to downplay our capabilities or been denied opportunities for growth and independence. In all of my conversations with (god), I've been supported and encouraged to reach out, to create, to grow and to shine. You have this same ability and (god) will help you.

> *"My thoughts are powerful and they are my creative tools. Every thought creates a form somewhere."* (GH)

> *"LIA (god) said, what you hear influences probability, if your mind can't conceive, if your heart can't feel, then the probability is low. The more you feel a possibility, the higher the probability that it will manifest."* (CW)

> *"Spirit (god): Your stream of consciousness does not just flow randomly. The stream bed is carefully arranged to direct the flow down the path of least resistance. I have placed each rock and pebble in just the right place. If you find your mind repeatedly coming back to one thing or another, pay attention. It is most likely a call to action. But instead of heeding that call, you get frustrated with these persistent thoughts and label the event as "being distracted" or "daydreaming." Then, you fight to redirect your mind back to whatever you believe you "should" be*

focused on. In reality, this redirection is the true distraction. If you would just stay with that thought, you would see where it is going and what it is about. When you consciously try to redirect your thinking, you are swimming against the current. Go with the flow and you will see how effortlessly you can float along. If you can do this with an open and easy heart, while letting go of expectations, you will be able to truly enjoy the adventure." (EM)

Whenever I share one of my dreams with (god), I receive an abundance of validation and an acknowledgement, that of course I ought to feel free to pursue whatever my heart or mind tells me. I know and feel (god's) support, whether it's through clarity, trust or as a confirmation of my value and it helps me take my next step toward making my dream a reality.

"I had a huge confirmation … my dreams … are coming true … that I need not do anything but live from pure presence … live from faith … live from divine inspiration." (BT)

"(Response from (god) regarding the experience of talking with (god)…) -- your newest tool for communicating with me will go on as you have raised your frequency to a much higher consciousness...all that is necessary to continue our conversation is that you create the time and space to allow this to happen...you will help the most, by continuing to walk in truth and living in love...as you often say regarding what your religion is...I have no religion…My religion is love…And every heart is my temple." (SL)

"I noticed by doing this practice every day … that awareness was built up … that my connection seemed deeper in a different way … I really enjoyed the moments of being present … asking questions… trusting and being open… knowing that all of the answers are already done…

talking with (god)

> *and that all I have to ever do is trust, let go, imagine lovingly, and let god."* (BT)

It's also valuable for me to remember that "free will" plays an integral part in the evolution of my relationship with (god).

> *"I believe that (god) gave each of us "free will". Without "free will" our stay here in this life, would not be 'normal', as we know it. (But) 'free will' should not be taken lightly."* (DM)

From time to time, I feel separate from (god) and from others. Fortunately, as I open my heart to (god) and allow (god) to speak to me, I come to remember the truth, that I am part of (god), part of the "oneness". Others have experienced this and shared their sense of this unity.

> *"My primary insight that was received from my conversation with GOD was that GOD is always present within me and surrounding me as this Oneness I can always trust is serving my highest good. I don't need to go anywhere else or do anything more. What I am a part of is fertile ground. There is no separating from me and Spirit or the Universe or GOD."* (JP)

I have also discovered on occasion, that what initially seemed to me to be a small thing, is not.

> *"What I've experienced over the past week might be small and trivial for some, but for me, it's a big shift in the way I've handled things in the past. Now I know I can share my frustrations (and victories) in quiet conversation instead of keeping them bottled up within and letting them fester. That's huge!"* (MW)

Although I have a lot of intellectual conversations, some of the most meaningful are those where I experience an emotional

talking with (god)

response, where I am able to free myself from my thinking mind and fall into my heart. It is a wonderful opportunity to give to myself and connect directly with (god's) love for me.

> *"I found great joy and felt and still am feeling so much love."* (PC)

> *"This new type of prayer was much more freeing and brought my faith to a more personal level. And, I found this new voice to be available now throughout the day and I was able to feel that comfort and peace in the middle of my walk."* (EG)

> *"The overwhelming message I received was one of unconditional love and protection on a daily basis. And I found that when I did my morning time of silence, breathing and openness to Spirit's messages, I was able to more easily return to that loving space throughout the day. The outside world was less harsh. Many times, I was unable to "hear" Spirit but felt enveloped in Spirit's bubble."* (DS)

I would have to say that my favorite messages from (god) are those that speak directly to me, and are personally about me. (God) is awesome at reminding me of who I am. That I am made of love. Being told this "makes my day" every time. I feel (god's) love so completely, that everything else disappears and I feel "home".

> *"Some messages are brief, others are longer and deeper. Here's one message I received. "I am so proud of you. You are a light beam among millions of light beams. You are worthy even when no one is telling you, even when you don't feel it, even when you are not giving, even when you are struggling or angry at the world. You are worthy, beautiful, beloved. I will keep telling you until you remember and feel Me. US!"* (DF)

75

talking with (god)

While these are all the steps in the process, there two additional elements that I feel are very important; habits and measures of success.

HABITS

The first relates to the creation of new habits. Any time you attempt to learn something new you are bound to experience challenges. One of these challenges may be whether to continue or not. It is often difficult to know for sure whether there is any real value in a new idea and it may take a period of time before there is any evidence to show for your efforts. If you don't get immediate "positive" results, you may be tempted to abandon the experience altogether. I would like to encourage you to give this process 30 days. This can be on any schedule that works for you.

Many experts who study habits, say that it takes more than two months before a new behavior or habit becomes automatic. Some experts seem to feel the exact number is 66 days. Others recommend that a person commit 21 straight days, which should create the habit, then follow this with another 90 days to cement the habit in place.

I think it's unreasonable to expect a prescribed plan of any sort will work for all people, no matter what the objective. I believe that if you begin and experience any connection with (god), there will be a bond created that will encourage you to continue. You'll *want* to keep going, because you'll feel (god's) presence and you'll sense something deep inside you that yearns for more. I believe there is actually nothing that I can say that will inspire you to talk with (god). That inspiration comes either from inside of you or inside of (god). All that I hope to do is to provide a nudge for you, to see for yourself what comes of having your own talks with (god).

talking with (god)

MEASURES OF SUCCESS

The second item I feel would benefit you to consider, before you continue, centers around your personal goal or goals for this process.

I believe that, we as humans, are trained to create or establish certain ideas about what we either expect or desire to happen. This is certainly my experience. It seems to happen whether I'm consciously thinking about it or not. I'll be doing something, and at times, notice a vague sense of dissatisfaction spread through me. If I'm aware enough, I'll stop and ask myself what is going on with me. Ordinarily, it's that I've set up an expectation and have in mind a specific way I want things to turn out. Below the surface, I've set up a "measure of success". Some part of me has automatically chosen this. I believe that I have enough established patterns and desires that I run on autopilot; the goal just pops into my mind without any conscious thought, and it is probably continuing from where I left off with my last goal.

Actually, thinking about and consciously deciding what you most desire, will assist you in your talks with (god). You can, of course, choose anything you want as a goal or measure, but spending some formal time creating a list or a plan, may provide a wonderful focus for you and serve as a starting place to begin your journey.

A brand-new friend, whom I am very grateful for, shared the following with me about what she chose as measures of success. I love her choices and it inspired me to think about and feel my way into creating my own list. Here's what she chose:

"Measures of Success-

--allowing myself to be authentic
--being detached from the judgement of others
--making a living at what brings me joy

talking with (god)

>--being of service to others
>--and feeling like I am contributing positively to other people's lives " (MP)

I encourage you to create your own list and see what develops. I've added space for this in the next chapter, where you will have a chance to try out this process for yourself .for when you arrive there.

Walking In
(your story)

talking with (god)

I wonder if you feel ready to get started on this journey? Or, if you already have a conversational relationship with (god), whether you're at a point of desiring to deepen your relationship? In the last chapter, I provided a lot of information and a basic outline of a process you could use and of course, if you feel ready to go, I certainly encourage you to do so. You can always come back to this chapter later if you desire.

However, if you feel you need a little more preparation, the framework that follows may be helpful to you.

This chapter is arranged in the style of a workbook, based on the steps I outlined earlier. Since this is *your* book, feel free to write in it, or, if you prefer, answer the questions in your journal or notebook, whatever feels wisest to you.

I'm going to ask you a series of questions and provide space for your responses. I believe that there is a significant value in answering these questions, because they can form a good jumping off point for you. You'll have spent time thinking through some fundamental issues, which will make it easier for you to begin your conversations with (god) or deepen the conversations you are already having. Please know that you are in charge here. You and (god) can make any decision work, and if you get stuck or need a refresher, you can always review any portion of this book.

Part of the value of answering these questions is for you to search inside yourself and pull out what is in your heart and mind. To bring it into the open, so you can decide consciously whether it reflects your truth or perhaps, it may provide you with an opportunity to make a change and shift your beliefs. It may also become a part of what you want to talk with (god) about and serve as the source of some wonderful conversations.

Okay, so, let's get started.

talking with (god)

If you and I were sitting together talking and trying to get to know each other, I'd want to have a little insight into your background, some reference points that would help me understand you as a person and as a spiritual being. The first chapter in this book allowed me to share a lot of *my* story with you. I tried to relay who I am through the events I told you about. I tried to give you an idea of what's important to me and, to an extent, why I believe I'm here on earth. I would love to know about you. I wish that I had the opportunity to actually talk with everyone that ever picks up this book -- to share stories, to know the person underneath the words and to connect with you in a way that we become "kindred spirits". I believe we are all kindred spirits and are part of one family.

When you answer these questions, please be as honest with yourself as you can. This is your personal life story. Wherever you are in your life right now, this is the place to start. Writing down your answers can be very freeing and provide a fresh opening for you. This whole process is about you. About the life you want to live and about what you want to create and experience. This is your chance to speak from your heart.

If you like the idea of writing your truth down in these answers and keeping all of what you write between you and (god), that's awesome.

But, if you prefer, you could imagine the idea that you and I are new friends, who have grown close because of a mutual desire to talk with (god). We are very comfortable with each other and sharing is free and easy. You know that I am interested in what you have to say and so you share what you have written with me, in hopes that your inner truth rises to the surface. If this idea feels comfortable to you, perhaps you'd like to imagine that as you write each answer, you are also telling me your story. You can imagine me sitting with you, nodding my head and occasionally asking you some follow-up question, so that I truly

talking with (god)

understand what you're telling me. If this sounds appealing to you, please feel free to use this approach.

Whatever you decide that is right for you, I honor your decision.

So, here are some questions for you. Of course, if the space provided isn't enough, find a way to finish your answers somewhere else. The important thing is to write 'all' of what feels 'right' to you.

One more thing you should know is that there are a lot of questions. I believe that there is merit to each one, but I also recognize that it might feel overwhelming to think you need to answer them all before you can get started. You don't. So, again, please realize that I am providing a framework and *you* are making the decisions. I want to remind you that there is no right way or wrong way to go about this, and for this to work well, it has to feel comfortable to you. You are in charge. If at any time you want to jump into having conversations with (god) and skip or come back to the questions, by all means, please do.

talking with (god)

PREPARATION

What name or names do you use for (god)?

_____
_____
_____
_____
_____
_____
_____
_____
_____
_____
_____
_____
_____
_____
_____
_____
_____
_____
_____
_____

talking with (god)

What is your religious or spiritual background?

_____
_____
_____
_____
_____
_____
_____
_____
_____
_____
_____
_____
_____
_____
_____
_____
_____
_____
_____
_____

talking with (god)

How would you describe your relationship with (god)?

_____

_____

_____

_____

_____

_____

_____

_____

_____

_____

_____

_____

_____

_____

_____

_____

_____

_____

_____

talking with (god)

Do you have a conversational relationship with (god)? By this I mean, do you talk with (god) *and* receive a response, which can be in any fashion – written, auditory, images, etc.? If so, what is it like?

_____
_____
_____
_____
_____
_____
_____
_____
_____
_____
_____
_____
_____
_____
_____
_____
_____
_____
_____
_____

talking with (god)

If you don't currently have a conversational relationship with
(god), do you believe it is possible to have one -- a conversation
where (god) speaks back to you?

_____

_____

_____

_____

_____

_____

_____

_____

_____

_____

_____

_____

_____

_____

_____

_____

_____

_____

_____

_____

talking with (god)

Is it a desire of yours to have a conversational relationship with (god)? (I don't want to assume that this is the case)

_____
_____
_____
_____
_____
_____
_____
_____
_____
_____
_____
_____
_____
_____
_____
_____
_____
_____
_____
_____
_____

talking with (god)

Do you believe that (god) wants to have a conversational relationship with you?

_____

_____

_____

_____

_____

_____

_____

_____

_____

_____

_____

_____

_____

_____

_____

_____

_____

_____

_____

_____

_____

talking with (god)

If you do, what actions on your part do you think you need to take to make/allow this to happen?

_____

_____

_____

_____

_____

_____

_____

_____

_____

_____

_____

_____

_____

_____

_____

_____

_____

_____

_____

_____

talking with (god)

If you are not sure whether (god) wants to have a conversational relationship with you or if (god) actually will have a conversational relationship with you, why do you feel the way you do?

_____

_____

_____

_____

_____

_____

_____

_____

_____

_____

_____

_____

_____

_____

_____

_____

_____

talking with (god)

Assuming that you want to have a conversation with (god) and believe that (god) wants this also, what do you *think will happen*?

_____
_____
_____
_____
_____
_____
_____
_____
_____
_____
_____
_____
_____
_____
_____
_____
_____
_____
_____

talking with (god)

Assuming that you want to have a conversation with (god) and believe that (god) wants this also, what do you *want to happen*?

_____
_____
_____
_____
_____
_____
_____
_____
_____
_____
_____
_____
_____
_____
_____
_____
_____
_____
_____
_____

talking with (god)

What obstacles do you feel may get in the way of having a conversation with (god)?

_____
_____
_____
_____
_____
_____
_____
_____
_____
_____
_____
_____
_____
_____
_____
_____
_____
_____
_____
_____
_____

talking with (god)

Do you feel any of the obstacles you mentioned will prevent you from having a conversation with (god)?

_____
_____
_____
_____
_____
_____
_____
_____
_____
_____
_____
_____
_____
_____
_____
_____
_____
_____
_____

talking with (god)

If so, which obstacles do you believe will get in the way?

_____
_____
_____
_____
_____
_____
_____
_____
_____
_____
_____
_____
_____
_____
_____
_____
_____
_____

talking with (god)

If you encounter these obstacles, what ideas do you have about ways you can overcome them?

_____
_____
_____
_____
_____
_____
_____
_____
_____
_____
_____
_____
_____
_____
_____
_____
_____
_____

talking with (god)

Do you have any fears about having a conversation with (god)?
If so, what are they?

_____

_____

_____

_____

_____

_____

_____

_____

_____

_____

_____

_____

_____

_____

_____

_____

_____

_____

talking with (god)

What might you be able to do to release these fears?

_____
_____
_____
_____
_____
_____
_____
_____
_____
_____
_____
_____
_____
_____
_____
_____
_____

talking with (god)

What are your intentions for your conversations?

_____

_____

_____

_____

_____

_____

_____

_____

_____

_____

_____

_____

_____

_____

_____

_____

_____

talking with (god)

What are your expectations for your conversations?

_____

_____

_____

_____

_____

_____

_____

_____

_____

_____

_____

_____

_____

_____

_____

_____

_____

_____

_____

talking with (god)

What topics would you like to talk about with (god)?

_____

_____

_____

_____

_____

_____

_____

_____

_____

_____

_____

_____

_____

_____

_____

_____

_____

talking with (god)

What time of day do you think would be best for your conversation(s)?

_____

_____

_____

_____

_____

_____

_____

_____

_____

_____

_____

_____

_____

_____

_____

_____

_____

talking with (god)

What location do you think would be the most beneficial for your conversation(s)?

_____

_____

_____

_____

_____

_____

_____

_____

_____

_____

_____

_____

_____

_____

_____

_____

_____

_____

talking with (god)

What ways work best for you to relax and calm yourself?

_____
_____
_____
_____
_____
_____
_____
_____
_____
_____
_____
_____
_____
_____
_____
_____
_____
_____
_____

talking with (god)

What instrumental music might aid in your relaxation?

_____
_____
_____
_____
_____
_____
_____
_____
_____
_____
_____
_____
_____
_____
_____
_____
_____
_____

talking with (god)

Are there specific breathing techniques that aid in your relaxation? If so, what are they?

_____

_____

_____

_____

_____

_____

_____

_____

_____

_____

_____

_____

_____

_____

_____

_____

_____

_____

_____

talking with (god)

What way or ways do you feel comfortable asking (god) to be present so you can have a conversation?

_____
_____
_____
_____
_____
_____
_____
_____
_____
_____
_____
_____
_____
_____
_____
_____
_____

talking with (god)

Do you see any value in expressing gratitude, in advance, for your conversation with (god)?
If so, what is the value to you?

_____
_____
_____
_____
_____
_____
_____
_____
_____
_____
_____
_____
_____
_____
_____
_____
_____
_____
_____

talking with (god)

How can you best set the stage for yourself for asking (god) questions and being open to hear/understand (god's) answers?

_____

_____

_____

_____

_____

_____

_____

_____

_____

_____

_____

_____

_____

_____

_____

_____

_____

_____

talking with (god)

Do you think there is a difference between asking questions from your mind versus your heart?

_____

_____

_____

_____

_____

_____

_____

_____

_____

_____

_____

_____

_____

_____

_____

_____

_____

talking with (god)

Do you feel there is a difference between listening to (god's) answers from your heart versus your mind?

_____

_____

_____

_____

_____

_____

_____

_____

_____

_____

_____

_____

_____

_____

_____

_____

_____

_____

_____

_____

talking with (god)

Are you comfortable recording what you receive from (god), in whatever way it shows up for you (a voice, words, thoughts, images…)?

_____
_____
_____
_____
_____
_____
_____
_____
_____
_____
_____
_____
_____
_____
_____
_____
_____
_____

talking with (god)

Do you see any value in recording what you receive from (god), so that you can review later?

_____

_____

_____

_____

_____

_____

_____

_____

_____

_____

_____

_____

_____

_____

_____

_____

_____

_____

_____

talking with (god)

DURING THE CONVERSATION

Do you hear (god's) voice? If so, what does it sound like to you?
If not, how do you feel about this?

_____

_____

_____

_____

_____

_____

_____

_____

_____

_____

_____

_____

_____

_____

_____

_____

_____

talking with (god)

Do you sense (god's) presence? If so, how does it make you feel? If not, do you feel there is a reason for this?

_____

_____

_____

_____

_____

_____

_____

_____

_____

_____

_____

_____

_____

_____

_____

_____

_____

_____

_____

talking with (god)

Are you comfortable speaking to (god)? If so, how do you feel about this? If not, why do you think you aren't comfortable?

_____

_____

_____

_____

_____

_____

_____

_____

_____

_____

_____

_____

_____

_____

_____

_____

_____

_____

_____

_____

talking with (god)

Once you've communicated with (god), do you receive a response? If so, what sort of response do you receive? If not, what do you think it means?

_____
_____
_____
_____
_____
_____
_____
_____
_____
_____
_____
_____
_____
_____
_____
_____
_____
_____
_____
_____

talking with (god)

Have you encountered any obstacles in either speaking with (god) or receiving a response from (god)? If so, what kind of obstacles did you encounter? If not, how does this feel to you?

_____
_____
_____
_____
_____
_____
_____
_____
_____
_____
_____
_____
_____
_____
_____
_____
_____
_____
_____

talking with (god)

If you are having conversations with (god), what do you think accounts for this (timing, location, frequency, openness on your part, desire…)?

_____

_____

_____

_____

_____

_____

_____

_____

_____

_____

_____

_____

_____

_____

_____

_____

_____

_____

talking with (god)

If you are not having conversations with (god), what do you think the issue(s) are that are preventing it (them) from happening? And, what do you think you can do about this?

_____

_____

_____

_____

_____

_____

_____

_____

_____

_____

_____

_____

_____

_____

_____

_____

_____

_____

_____

talking with (god)

Has your practice of having conversations with (god) become a routine that you do on a pretty regular schedule? Does this work best for you?

_____

_____

_____

_____

_____

_____

_____

_____

_____

_____

_____

_____

_____

_____

_____

_____

_____

_____

_____

_____

talking with (god)

Is your practice more random than an established routine (not on any regular schedule)? Does this work best for you?

---

talking with (god)

Is there anything preventing you from feeling open to have conversations with (god)? If so, what stands in your way?

_____

_____

_____

_____

_____

_____

_____

_____

_____

_____

_____

_____

_____

_____

_____

_____

_____

_____

talking with (god)

If there are things standing in the way, of your conversations, what actions do you think you can take to release them?

_____

_____

_____

_____

_____

_____

_____

_____

_____

_____

_____

_____

_____

_____

_____

_____

_____

_____

_____

talking with (god)

Do you feel committed to this process? If not, what issues are impacting your commitment?

_____
_____
_____
_____
_____
_____
_____
_____
_____
_____
_____
_____
_____
_____
_____
_____
_____
_____
_____
_____

talking with (god)

Are you giving yourself permission to be open to moving whatever direction you feel you need in order to have conversations with (god)?

_____
_____
_____
_____
_____
_____
_____
_____
_____
_____
_____
_____
_____
_____
_____
_____
_____
_____
_____

talking with (god)

What are your personal measurements of success or, if you
have not set any, what would you want them to be?

_____

_____

_____

_____

_____

_____

_____

_____

_____

_____

_____

_____

_____

_____

_____

_____

_____

_____

_____

talking with (god)

It's very important for you to feel you have absolute freedom to make all decisions. This is, after all, your personal experience; yours and (god)'s. I realize it may feel overwhelming and you might be saying, "I wish I could read one of Rob's conversations, so that I had an idea of what mine might look like". If this is the case, I encourage you to turn to Appendix (I), for a recent conversation I had with Lia.

Remember, we're all very different people and approach things from many angles and in different ways at different times. If something isn't working for me, I shift and change directions. I'd encourage you to do the same.

talking with (god)

Appendices TABLE OF CONTENTS

APPENDIX (A)

Why It's Important to Me to Speak My Truth

I wanted to include this section of the book because of how profoundly I have been changed through my talking with (god). I have shifted a great deal during my conversational years since 1997 and my inner spirit has expanded. So much so, that I have a strong desire to share what I've received. That is the main reason I've written this book.

The following are a sampling of the "intentions" (desires I feel I want to act upon) *because of my relationship with (god)*. Each of these statements uses the word "them", referring to "those people in my life with whom I want to share" and "those I want to remind about truths I believe in".

I want to help them:

See that they can love themselves and that nothing needs to stand in the way of this awareness.

Realize that there are valuable gifts and learnings that happen within *every* experience in their lives.

Realize that *everyone* is beautiful, loved, valued, worthy, free willed, awesome and is a radiantly divine being.

Realize that we all have a choice about how to view and experience our lives and we can *release* what we've been told and *embrace* what (god), the divine tells and shows us.

See that *everyone* can talk with (god) and tell (god) how they *truly* feel, without any fear, and that it is a two-way dialogue and that (god) will answer all of their questions, if they are open. And, if they choose to listen, to hear the "good news" that (god) wants what they want or something even better.

talking with (god)

See the value and the accountability of "testing" (god) and literally "tracking" the results.

Release any teachings they've received which no longer serve them or restrict their freedom to explore their most intimate relationship directly with (god), so they come to *know* (god) and *trust* (god) and *rely* on (god).

Recognize from my explanations how a conversational relationship works, by connecting them directly to the process.

Understand that the process I am sharing allows and encourages them to find their *own* path, to learn, discover and reveal *their* own truth.

Experience this life in all of its beauty and to share that with all others, because I want to follow (god's) lead and "Just love them. Just love them as they are, without need to change them".

talking with (god)

If you feel called to write out a list of your own reasons to speak your truth, here's some space for that:

_____

_____

_____

_____

_____

_____

_____

_____

_____

_____

_____

_____

_____

_____

_____

_____

_____

_____

_____

_____

talking with (god)

APPENDIX (B)

Benefits I've Received from Talking with (god)

I feel loved.

I feel listened to.

I feel cared for.

I feel respected.

I feel "known".

I can talk about anything.

(God) will always repeat anything I ask about or say it in another way, so that I understand it.

(God) never speaks in a harsh or judgmental way.

I can come to a conversation in any mood; angry, sad, excited, wondering or needy, and I am always accepted and loved.

(God) is always responsive and when I don't hear I know it is because of me…which is okay. I know I'm just not able, in that moment, to slow down enough to hear, so (god) gives me room, so that when I am settled, I can hear.

What I receive is so simple and profound, which allows me to make major shifts in my life and in my consciousness.

(God) guides me, letting me figure things out for myself, because the new awarenesses I discover in this way "stick with me".

I feel (god's) sweetness and know, because I feel it deep inside of me, that (god) loves me, always and forever.

talking with (god)

(God) has a wonderful sense of humor and appreciates mine.

I ask lots of questions and receive answers, as long as I give (god) and myself a chance.

Sometimes the answers are not at all what I expect and often move me in the opposite direction from what I anticipated.

I am often surprised and frequently challenged, but I always know that whatever is given to me is the truth, because I can *feel* it.

I am guided to relax and calm myself and accept the beautiful feeling of just breathing.

I am offered insights and it is up to me whether I accept them. I am never forced, coerced or manipulated into accepting any suggestion. It is always on my terms.

I am offered new ways of looking at familiar thoughts and ideas in my life (like the concept of "PEMSE," Physical, Emotional, Mental, Spiritual and Ego).

(god) is my sanctuary, my refuge, my center of peace, which is especially so when the world turns chaotic and fractured.

I've received wisdom that feels true to me, despite the fact that much of it contradicts what 'culture' teaches.

I receive reassurance when my doubts creep in and overwhelm me.

My heart is opened wide in (god's) presence, and if I allow it, I can release everything and disappear into oneness with (god)…*Ahhhh.*

talking with (god)

If you feel called to write out a list of your own benefits you've received or would like to receive, here's some space for that:

_____

_____

_____

_____

_____

_____

_____

_____

_____

_____

_____

_____

_____

_____

_____

_____

_____

_____

_____

_____

_____

_____

talking with (god)

Appendix (C) Beta Test Group Information

List of Religious or Spiritual Backgrounds

The responses received from the Beta group are depicted in word clouds. Google says a word cloud is "an image composed of words used in a particular text or subject, in which the size of each word indicates its frequency or importance." So, the more often a specific word appears in the responses, the bigger and bolder it appears in the word cloud.

In this word cloud, you see that Catholic is the biggest and boldest word in the cloud. That lets you know that most of the beta testers had a Catholic background. Conversely, Mormon, Quaker, Unitarian, and Congregational are all very small in the cloud which indicates that not many of the beta testers came from those faith backgrounds.

Appendix (D) Beta Test Group Information
List of Name Used for (god)

talking with (god)

Appendix (E) Beta Test Group Information
List of Obstacles Anticipated

Physical, Mental, Ego Obstacles

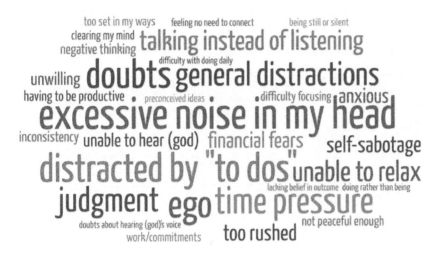

too set in my ways   feeling no need to connect   being still or silent
clearing my mind   talking instead of listening
negative thinking
difficulty with doing daily
unwilling **doubts** general distractions
having to be productive • preconceived ideas • • difficulty focusing anxious
excessive noise in my head
inconsistency unable to hear (god) financial fears   self-sabotage
distracted by "to dos" unable to relax
lacking belief in outcome doing rather than being
judgment ego time pressure
doubts about hearing (god)'s voice   not peaceful enough
work/commitments   too rushed

Emotional Obstacles

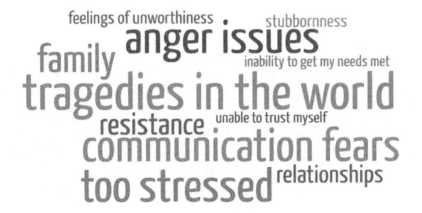

feelings of unworthiness •   stubbornness
family **anger issues**
inability to get my needs met
tragedies in the world
resistance • unable to trust myself
communication fears
too stressed relationships

talking with (god)

Spiritual Obstacles

don't have relationship with (god)
lack of faith and trust
afraid of the answers
hard to surrender
difficulty with (god) being eternal
belief I should be able to figure things out for myself
wondering if it's really (god)'s voice
struggle with faith versus fear hidden beliefs feeling my issues not significant
loss of faith uncommitted
our human story not open to the process
need a reason to live accepting relationship with (god)

talking with (god)

Appendix (F) Beta Test Group information
List Summary of Topics Anticipated

Physical, Mental Ego Topics

tithing

lose weight

more discipline

repair and build my business

abundance supporting myself

healing the earth finances

how do I find health help in getting a book out

sickness (and fear of illness)

stop being ego and fear driven

everyday life concerns

alternate ways to get aerobic exercise

Emotional Topics

more compassion

am I doing right by my children

more peace

understand the difference between persistence and resistance   deal with self-doubt and self-sabotage

guidance in personal relationships

sexual balance   being authentic   release control

special relationship

open my heart   struggle with aloneness   changing me   understand life

other relationships

let go of anger ways to manifest or deepen love

help other with healing   more positive and less negative love fearlessly

accept others   healing relationships

forgiveness   how to be more generous

how to be more joyful   understanding the difference between romantic and universal love

help with anxiety and fear

how to stay positive   needing others to feel whole

deeper gratefulness loving and giving

how to deal with loss

talking with (god)

Spiritual Topics

finding meaning in the pandemic

insight when am I going to do what I came here for?
deeper understanding of how to live more fully

how to manifest
deeper connection to (god)
how to listen and hear

what I most need to know at this time

understand my resistance to the spiritual process

life purpose

how to get out of my own way   significance of past lives   learning to trust (god)

how to co-create heaven on earth I best serve

how can I best serve

help with sense of separation

surrender
experience self-actualization

living in union with (god)   how best to spend time
do we create our own reality?   know the mind of (god)

help putting faith into action

be the best me

APPENDIX (G) Beta Test Group Information

List of Beta Tester Question

1. Briefly describe your religious/spiritual background.

2. What name or names do YOU use for (god)?

3. Do you already have a conversational relationship with (god)?

4. How close do you feel to (god)?

5. Are there any obstacles or challenges you imagine will interfere with your conversations with (god)? If there are, what are they?

6. What do you *think* you will experience during this process?

7. What would you most like to happen during this process?

8. What two or three topics would you most like to talk about with (god)?

talking with (god)

APPENDIX (H)

Ways Through the Noise

Here are some suggestions in case you are having difficulty coming into a quiet space within and stilling the chatter in your mind.

Ask (god) For Help
Surprisingly, I overlooked this very obvious answer for years, despite, or perhaps because of its simplicity.

Gandhi Approach
Become nonresistant and non-violent in your approach, recognizing the appearance of all thoughts, but letting them all pass by you easily.

Catch and Release
Similar to the GANDHI approach, but when thoughts arise, hold them gently in your mind, acknowledge them, thank them for coming, then *consciously* release them, knowing you can address them later, if necessary.

Broken Record
Use a "mantra" (word or set of words), repeating them over and over, filling the space in your mind and directing your mantra toward your desire. For example: You could repeat a mantra like, "(God) I am open to hearing your beautiful voice".

Music
Listen to soothing music (without lyrics) and relax into the sound, but not so much that you fall asleep.

Focused Physical Relaxation
Concentrate on each body part, starting at your toes, first tightening, then letting go completely of any tension. Work your

talking with (god)

way up your body to the top of your head. Once there, enjoy the release.

Other Method of Your Choice
Use any method that offers you a way to gently let go of your active, conscious mind and provides relaxation and open space.

talking with (god)

APPENDIX (I)

One of My Conversations

This conversation took place on the morning of June 14, 2020. At this point I'd finished the first draft of this book and was struggling a bit with my hopes and dreams about it. Part of me wants it to be a success, so that all the folks who read it, come to believe it is possible for them to have their own conversations with (god), where they receive their own answers and find their own direction. Another part of me feels that I need to let go of any desire for a specific outcome and allow (god)/spirit to guide the whole process. And another part of me is unsure what to hope for.

This last is the part that feels a certain weight. It's the part that is quite unsure what to do if it is a big commercial success or goes nowhere. I recognize the voices speaking these words as a combination of my ego and my mind. They are tag-teaming the rest of me and keeping us somewhat off balance. I feel a strong need for clarity. I've actually tried several times to have a conversation with (god) and gain the clarity I desire, but without success. I have to remind myself that I will only be able to hear clearly when I quiet myself and breathe and open my heart and ask for help, knowing it's always there for me and being grateful, in advance for it. So, I sit and open and wait and here is what happened…

Lia encouraged me to be honest and say what I was feeling. This is really hard to do, partially because I don't always know what I'm feeling and also it takes more courage than I sometimes have. I know by now that giving in completely is always the smart thing for me to do.

Because we'd been talking about this same subject on June 12, the conversation picks up from there. For your benefit I'm labeling our parts as "R": for Rob and "L": for Lia, one of my

talking with (god)

names for (god), who is my ethereal female voice representing "Love In Action". When I'm writing my conversations I only use lower case letters because it's the fastest way for me. I often have a hard enough time keeping up with the conversation as it is, let alone spending time writing upper case letters and punctuation. For your benefit, I've typed out our conversation in a reader-friendly version. I encourage you to write in whatever style you enjoy and makes it easiest for you.

What I love most about this conversation is it offers me a way to feel "weightless". Awesome!

R: I want to let go. I want to be free. I want to release all the stuff I've been holding on to for all of these years.

L: That would be awesome.

R: What do I need to do?

L: I know you think it's complicated, but it really isn't. It's a simple shift in perception. You have all the evidence that you need already. Can you sense that?

R: Yes.

L: Everything is a shift of perception in the world of change (whether it's release or embrace)

R: So, what do I do?

L: Try to accept the idea that "everything" that happens in your life, brings you closer and closer to your true self. Does that feel true to you?

R: Yes.

talking with (god)

L: So, what if everything is real? What if there aren't separate things that belong in only one location and that 'everything' is part of the ONE?

R: That would change things.

L: How do you mean that?

R: That everything I experience is part of a WHOLE, rather than separate parts, some of which I label as "good" or "bad".

L: And how would this change your experience of each event in your life?

R: All things that I experience would be potentially valuable to me, because they all are a part of my whole experience here.

L: Why do you say potentially?

R: Because for them to be actually valuable, I'd have to see them that way. So often now I evaluate my experiences and assign them a relative value. There is a wide range, spanning from very bad to very good. For me to see all of my experiences as valuable, I would have to turn their potential value into actual value.

L: And how would you do that?

R: I'd have to change my perception of them. Isn't that what you were saying to me before?

L: Yes. Shall we look at an example?

R: Yes please. That (almost always) helps me. Sometimes I'm too stubborn or distracted to pay attention. I realize that if I don't understand what you are telling me, that some part of me isn't

148

talking with (god)

ready for the answer…and if I can, letting that be okay is good for me.

L: Yes, being gentle with yourself is really important.

R: What would be a good example to use?

L: What are you afraid of at this particular moment?

R: That this book won't get out there because I lack the skills necessary to make it happen.

L: At first blush I know this makes sense to you, but think a little deeper for me.

R: Do you mean, I could hire a professional marketing firm to do this for me?

L: Yes, that's certainly one direction and it might be the choice you make. What else?

R: I could ask everyone I know and ask them to tell the folks they know…I could give out lots of copies and ask folks to spread the word.

L: But ultimately, you struggle with the "idea" that it won't happen…is that true?

R: Yes, that no matter what, it won't be successful (commercially) -- which means that I won't have been able to help others, so they can have their own conversations with you (which I believe could favorably change their lives).

L: So, this is all up to you? Is that the underlying feeling you have in this moment?

talking with (god)

R: Yes, it is. Despite being told by others that this is a good and worthy thing I'm doing, I still have feelings of doubt about moving it out into the world, like I want to.

L: You don't feel in control of the outcome?

R: No, not really

L: And that bothers you?

R: Yes. This is a real passion for me. I know personally what this could mean to someone, because of what it's meant to me. I would love for others to be able to experience this same thing. Is that wrong?

L: You know there is no such thing as "right" or "wrong", because everyone sees the world differently. Right and wrong are relative terms and we've talked about that for a long time. I hear what you are saying though. You desire that others have the option of choosing to have a relationship with me. Do you realize that you are not the only route for them to travel?

R: Yes, of course. But I feel that this is part of my mission here on earth. I've received so much insight from you, and I'd like to share it with others.

L: You realize that you already are, right? You felt it would be important to share about this process that's worked for you (and you did) and then you felt that writing a book would be a great idea (so you are), and then you felt like it was important to involve others in the process as beta-testers and so you asked (and they accepted). And you know everything is in place to create this book and have it available on Amazon, so that anyone, anywhere in the world can buy it. So, you ARE sharing it with others, aren't you? I tell you the truth…you will accomplish your mission. Do you feel this as the truth?

talking with (god)

R: Yes.

L: But, you want more, don't you?

R: Yes.

L: What else do you want?

R: I want folks who are happy and folks who are sad to be able to come to you and for it to change their lives (like it has mine).

L: What about what they want? Do you believe that when someone has a need and seeks to fill it, that they will find what they seek?

R: No, not always.

L: So, tell me how you see it working?

R: Sometimes people need to be offered something -- then they can choose.

L: Like your book?

R: Yes, like my book.

L: And what happens if they don't find your book?

R: I guess they either search for something else or they continue feeling the way they do.

L: Is part of your motivation to provide for them, to be an answer to their questions?

R: Yes.

L: How heavy is that weight?

talking with (god)

R: Really, really heavy.

L: How does that feel?

R: Even though it feels like I'm doing this for all of the right reasons, it feels oppressive too, like I can't be happy until the book is a success...and this feeling is burdensome (and has been with me for so long).

L: Would you like to be free from this weight?

R: Yes, very much so. How do I do that?

L: By shifting your perception and trusting me. By trusting the way the world works.

R: I was with you about trusting you, but when you added, trusting the way the world works, you lost me because I've seen the way the world works and it's often harsh (and a lot of other negative words)

L: Ahh, but there's the crux of the issue. You've become accustomed to seeing only the 'surface level', so of course, you are skeptical and find it disturbing. What I'm asking you to do (sharing with you) is to see *below the surface*.

R: How?

L: Everything in your world is connected. Everyone in your world is connected. Think about the aspen tress...they appear separate above the surface...but they are intimately connected below the surface.

There is no real separation. You view the world with human eyes. Even on your very best day, your most profound and insightful day, you see only a tiny fraction of the truth, that all

talking with (god)

things (people, events, nature…) are connected, parts of the whole.

Everything is valuable, worthwhile, beautiful. Everything is learning, sensing, creating, experiencing…everything is doing what it chooses.

You are trying to make sense of it all. I'm telling you, that as a human, this is not possible. If your humanity was released, you could see the truth and there are those who, for moments, truly let go and sense the truth (without trying to understand it intellectually and they see the truth).

Since you can't see every connection, you use your senses (physical, emotional, mental, spiritual and ego, too) to evaluate and decide if what you do see is right or wrong.

R: I don't and can't see enough of the picture to know the truth…that's what you're saying to me?

L: Yes, how does that feel to you?

R: Like the truth. And based on what you said, I recognize that I can't see the whole picture. So, this all comes down to faith and trust, doesn't it?

L: Yes. You either do or you don't have faith and then trust. What you choose, creates your perception of your world.

R: Circling back…all of my concerns regarding the success of the book…what about them and the weight they create for me?

L: Their weight is dependent on your choice about how to see the world. If you choose the surface level, you will feel their weight. If you choose the below the surface level, they will be weightless. Having faith and trusting that all is well under the surface, creates a peaceful heart and allows you to surrender all

talking with (god)

of your concerns about outcomes. You are free, because you know everything is connected and part of the one.

R: Thank you for this (drawing of a heart). I want this. I want to feel weightless. Please help me shift my perceptions so I am filled with faith and trust.

L: How you choose it to be, it will be. I love (drawing of a heart) you. Thanks for asking me about this.

R: Thank you for the visual images.

<not shown here in this book, but drawn in my notebook where my conversations are recorded – just described in words so you'd know what appeared in my notebook>.

(drawing of storm clouds…raining down into an angry ocean…with fierce waves…and yet as you see further below the surface you see that it is placid and peaceful)

then

(drawing of a grove of aspen trees which appear separate above the surface and yet when viewed from below the surface, they are interconnected and share one root system)

Great visuals to remember both principles

R: So, all of my concerns are the storm above the surface, right?

L: Yes.

R: If I choose to shift my perceptions (what I'm looking at or consider to be true for me) I can control (decide for myself) the way to view my life…for example: from storm thinking (above the surface) to peaceful thinking (below the surface)

talking with (god)

L: Yes.

R: I can choose to have FAITH in you and the plan (oneness and connectedness) and this creates TRUST between us and I can choose to SURRENDER my tightly held thoughts of OUTCOMES and feel WEIGHTLESS, right?

L: Yes, my love. This and so much more.

R: Thank you. I love you (drawing of a heart).

talking with (god)

APPENDIX (J)

Contact with the Author (Website info)

I've been thinking about writing this book for many years, but certain fears have prevented me from actively pursuing it until now. Maybe fears have stood in your way, keeping you from important things too. I would like to see if we can overcome some of our fears together and find ways to strengthen ourselves, then grow fully into the radiant beings I believe we all are.

talking with (god)

In one of my recent conversations with Lia, we talked about measures of success. I found that the ones I had previously believed in were losing their appeal to me. I felt a shift take place, one that both surprised and delighted me. Somehow the words changed and took a new shape, becoming "aims and intentions". While I still feel that "measures of success" has merit, I've come to see that there is a subtle, yet significant difference that alters my approach to life and my subsequent happiness. Shifting my focus to "aims and intentions", I feel an openness and freedom and I sense that if I don't accomplish an aim or an intention, it will still be okay.

So, I'd like to share with you that an aim and intention of mine is to provide you with a way to learn more about the talking with (god) process through a weekly blog. I want to communicate with readers who are interested in knowing more, in asking questions and sharing some of their experiences. I have created a website for this purpose:

www.messagesforinspiration.com

My aim is to share some of my conversations with (god) and the insights and observations I have received and also to provide an opportunity for blog readers to respond with comments and questions. My plan is to read all of the comments and respond with a summary answer, unless I have the time to answer individually. I hope you will be led to join in a dialogue with me and others who are on this journey.

Also, if you are interested in reading some of my other books, you will find direct links on my website to Amazon, where they may be ordered.

Made in the USA
Middletown, DE
04 November 2020